Praise for the First]

"I've done the scientific research to establish why stories are so powerful for human communications. Jim's book is an excellent practical guide to how to effectively use them."

—Kendall Haven, story strategist, author, and master storyteller

"Heroic brands make the customer the hero of their brand story. *StoryBranding* makes the journey easy, predictable, and profitable."

—Dave Lakhani, author of *Persuasion: The Art of Getting What You Want*

"Jim uses humor and stories brilliantly to provide a roadmap for making your brand stand out. Everyone loves a great story—listen to his tales and let everyone love your brand. This is a book that is tough to put down."

—Sal Sredni, owner and CEO of TradeStation Group

"*StoryBranding* resonates just like a great story. Like the brand-building process itself, Jim's analogy is part vision-quest, part how-to, and completely engaging. More than a book, this workbook is a must-read for those brands that want to be part of the Participation Economy."

—Lisa Colantuono, copartner, AAR Partners; adjunct advertising
professor, New York Institute of Technology

"How does a brand become one seen as the right brand? The one about which customers feel 'My brand gets me'? It's challenging, but we know it can be done, because the best customers feel it, and even say things like, 'But my brand is different.' *StoryBranding* is a terrific read for those who want to make this happen."

—Tom Collinger, associate dean of Integrated Marketing,
Northwestern University

"If someone asked me for one book on how to build an enduring brand, I would direct them to *StoryBranding*. Jim Signorelli takes you on a step-by-step process of how to use the power of storytelling to help brands connect emotionally with their consumers."

—Larry Kelly, Clinical professor of advertising, University of Houston

"Jim Signorelli's *StoryBranding* is intriguing. To economists, advertising conveys information about a product or service. A story can help to fix an image of the product or create an association in the mind of the consumer. What better approach is there for political advertising, where each politician has a story and, in the end, is the story?"

—Robert Brusca, PhD, chief economist, Fact and Opinion Economics

"It is almost too good to be true that this book has finally been written. Jim Signorelli blends years of wisdom with the magic of story in a format that is so accessible it makes me cry that I didn't have it twenty years ago."

—Annette Simmons, bestselling author of *Whoever Tells the Best Story Wins* and *The Story Factor*

"All marketers should read Jim's book, especially those who haven't embraced storytelling. It not only drives home the efficacy of storytelling, but also offers a roadmap for leveraging this tool to uniquely communicate the human essence of a brand. Thought-provoking and useful book."

—Dennis Dunlap, CEO, American Marketing Association

"Jim Signorelli travels where few advertising/marketing books have gone before. He masterfully decodes brand storytelling without ever going astray from the business conversation. Therein lies his genius, as Signorelli remains grounded in a story we can all relate to: delivering a functional framework for how brands can speak truth, create culture, and transform the world. An essential must-read!"

—Michael Margolis, President, GetStoried.com, author of *Believe Me*

"We all use stories to communicate with each other—families, friends, or business associates. Jim has captured the essence of how to tell a good story that not only resonates with the listener but drives home the message in a clear and concise fashion."

—Russ Umphenour, CEO, FOCUS Brands

"*StoryBranding* stands out from the crowd of 'how to use stories' books by focusing on the structure of story itself. *StoryBranding* shows how story logic, even more than stories themselves, can illuminate the dynamic nature of the branding process. It has already changed how I will approach defining and communicating my own brand."

—Doug Lipman, storytelling coach, Storydynamics.com

STORY
BRANDING 2.0

JIM SIGNORELLI

STORY
BRANDING 2.0

CREATING STAND-OUT BRANDS
THROUGH THE POWER OF STORY

JIM SIGNORELLI

RIVER GROVE
BOOKS

This publication is designed to provide accurate and authoritative information in regard to the subject matter covered. It is sold with the understanding that the publisher and author are not engaged in rendering legal, accounting, or other professional services. Nothing herein shall create an attorney-client relationship, and nothing herein shall constitute legal advice or a solicitation to offer legal advice. If legal advice or other expert assistance is required, the services of a competent professional should be sought.

Published by River Grove Books
Austin, TX
www.rivergrovebooks.com

Distributed by River Grove Books

Design and composition by Greenleaf Book Group
Cover design by Story-Lab Publications

Publisher's Cataloging-in-Publication data is available.

Print ISBN: 978-1-63299-655-8

eBook ISBN: 978-1-62634-032-9

Second Edition

To Joan, my story's hero

One eye sees, the other eye feels.

—Paul Klee

Contents

FOREWORD

Human beings are story-seeking creatures. Since the dawn of civilization, stories have guided us, inspired us and healed us. Now because of Jim Signorelli, stories will change the way we market, forever.

Branding is often seen as a mystery story. Marketers acting more like detectives looking for clues to their customers and motives for why they buy. Jim Signorelli solves the riddle by providing a powerful and intuitive process that replaces mystery with mastery. Both a descriptive and prescriptive book on art and science of storytelling, StoryBranding 2.0 ushers in the next chapter in business communication.

Signorelli is a marvelous storyteller blessed with the right dose of wit, the right amount of words, and infinite wisdom. With these gifts he takes us on his own adventure story where he wrestles the behemoth we call branding and is victorious in building a new process for getting to your story, which he says and I agree, is the foundation of your brand. He also sends old ideas running like the *unique selling proposition* offering instead a unique telling proposition-your story.

His six Cs takes the reader from adventure to action story as Signorelli puts theory into fast-paced practice giving you the tools to build your own genuine and I-can't–put-it-down-page-turning story. This speaks to the power of this book; that it teaches us actually what to say rather than just how to say it.

In this way Jim shows us how to turn buyers into believers and brands into best sellers.

And the plot thickens. People are brands who wish to be engaged. That's when this fresh and simple framework turns love story as you discover that his process is also a personal branding and selling tool for you. You will discover, as I did, not only your StoryBrand but also yourself.

Finally, like all great storytellers, Signorelli tells plenty of them. That's why his book is not only my desk at work but also my nightstand at home. I have made it required reading at my consultancy BrightHouse and have read it out loud to my wife and children. The message can't be amplified enough—We are all once upon a time stories searching for happily ever after's.

What I love most about the story Jim wrote is that as brilliant and courageous as he is, he never claims to be the hero. That's because he knows you are. His research proves that your story can turn a brand into a stand, a point of difference into a point of view and customers into returning characters through out the life of your brand.

Please join me in adding a seventh C to Jim Signorelli's sea changing work. Congratulations.

—Joey Reiman, author of *The Story Of Purpose*

REINTRODUCTION

I cannot begin to explain how thrilled I was when I received a finished copy of my book from my publisher. It signaled the end. No more hiding from the rest of the world on weekends. No more contorted writing postures in airplane seats. No more rewrites or punctuation lessons from my editor.

I'm finally done!

So I thought.

I failed to anticipate something that would happen soon after the book was distributed. Specifically, I failed to consider that I would get a lot of questions from readers, answers to which would go beyond what I had originally written:

"How does this apply to personal branding?"

"Can StoryBranding be applied to personal selling?"

"How can I use this for my furniture store/pizzeria/real estate small business?"

"Is this a planning process that is better for entrepreneurs than corporations?"

Each question fired up new temptations to update my original manuscript. Obviously, that fire got too big to extinguish.

StoryBranding is a planning tool. As a process, it is used before any selling message is devised, whether that message be in the form of a story, an exposition, a PR release, a resume, or any other form of persuasive communication. It is more about how a convincing message should be blueprinted. This time around, I thought it better to suggest this on the cover than to influence someone to buy the book for the wrong reasons.

Throughout the book, I do discuss ways in which the message could or should be told, drawing on some important principles of story. But my primary intent is to help readers determine what to say (or not say) instead of how to say it. StoryBranding is, therefore, an approach, a discipline, and a philosophy that draws its purpose from the purpose of stories. It asks readers to think of themselves as authors instead of salespeople. Both professions intend to sell ideas. But I contend, as does history, that authors do a much better job of getting people to adopt their points of view. Understanding why is something that many books on selling, marketing, and/or advertising overlook.

While updating the first edition, I've also replaced some drawings with more informative graphics that better explain the tools of Story-Branding. My All-Star designer cast is headed up by Joe Pryzbylski who designed the 6Cs infographic as well as the bold new cover. Joe's creativity is as boundless as his determination to excel. Additionally, he puts "fun" into the creative process. Thanks also goes to Joanna Worthington, who designed each of the 12 archetype infographics. Joanna is one of the more insightful designers that I have had the pleasure of working with during my career.

Finally, I've added ten essays taken from our agency's blog, blog.eswstorylab.com. These add to what you will have learned in the text. But feel free to skip ahead, as they collectively summarize the key points.

Gratefully, there would be no need for a revision if the first book had been a flop. I have many to thank for the fact that it wasn't, including my publisher Greenleaf Book Group and Axiom Book Awards for the gold medal they awarded me. But topping the list of people I am most grateful to (and for) is Joan, my wife, best friend, muse, and endless source of encouragement.

NOTE TO THE READER

Countless books on the subject of branding are available, each with their own definitions of branding. To make certain we are using the same frame of reference, I thought it best to provide the definition of branding that I'll be using throughout this book. But first, and to fully understand my definition, I have to provide two other definitions, one for *product* and the other for *brand*. Without products and brands, branding doesn't matter. It wouldn't exist. Furthermore, *product* and *brand* are often mistaken for the same thing. They are certainly related, but in the same way a house is related to a home.

Whole papers have been written on the differences between products and brands. If my definitions seem more plain-spoken than scholastic, that's intentional. To get the full benefit of this book's content, you'll only need to know the essential differences.

- A product is simply something that is bought to perform a function. For example, a hammer is a product used to pound nails. I also lump services into the category of products since they, too, perform functions. Thus, I see carpentry, or the service of constructing things out of wood, as a product.

- A brand, on the other hand, is the designation that the sellers of a given product use to distinguish the product they sell from others. "Acme" may be the designation used to distinguish one seller's hammers from the sellers of competing hammers. Brands can also describe a family of products sold by a seller. Thus, "Acme," in addition to being the designation for a given hammer, could also be used to designate a line of hand tools, such as screwdrivers, wrenches, or pliers.

"Branding" then, from the perspective of the seller, is the process of assigning and associating certain meanings to brands.

Assigned meanings are those created by the seller in order to help us tell brands part. These meanings are communicated through the brand's name, logo, shape, size, and other physical product features unique to the brand. Going back to our hammer example, assigned meanings for Acme hammers help us to know that an Acme hammer is different than an Ace hammer. Trademarks often protect assigned meanings so that when someone buys an Acme hammer, they can be assured of buying the real thing.

Associative meanings consist of connotations we have for a given brand. Unlike assigned meanings, they are subjective thoughts and feelings and are solely dependent upon the buyer's exposure to and/or experience with the brand. Another key difference from assigned meanings is that associative meanings cannot be controlled by the seller. Sellers can only attempt to control whether one hammer is perceived as better than another, or that one hammer really does makes one feel more like a real carpenter than a do-it-yourselfer.

The real challenge of branding comes about from the need to influence associative meanings. No matter what the brand, the goal of branding is to optimally influence associative meanings that will result in marketing success. (Spoiler alert: marketing success is traditionally measured in terms of sales. As you'll see, this measure can be misleading.)

To achieve this goal, one can use any number of approaches, models, and disciplines. Many of them organize thinking and pose questions that must be answered. But the weakness inherent in any branding process is often not easily discerned until it's too late and too costly. Insights are overlooked, opportunities are missed, or the wrong problems are solved.

This book is about a very different branding approach, one that ensures a thorough and thoughtful process for establishing effective brand identities. We call this process StoryBranding. As with any planning model, there can be no guarantees that it will always work and for all brands. However, StoryBranding, by its very nature, will definitely stimulate your creativity while triggering ideas that would otherwise go uncaptured. It will give you a step-by-step method for developing your brand's identity, the way authors develop their story characters. And it will do this without the need for extensive experience with marketing or storytelling.

This book is divided into three parts. Part I, The Birth of a Notion, provides the background you'll need to fully benefit from the StoryBranding process. Here you'll learn how this process evolved from a personal experience that enlightened me to cast aside many of the branding tools I learned as a college undergraduate, a graduate student, and throughout my thirty-plus-year career as an advertising executive working for some of the largest agencies and clients in the country. In Part I you'll also be introduced to the elements of story that provide the foundation on which the StoryBranding process is built.

By the time you reach Part II, you will know why story structure serves as the engine for this branding process. And hopefully you'll see for yourself that this engine can take you further than you ever imagined possible, and with minimal effort. But unlike other books that extol the benefits of seeing brands as stories, I wanted to make certain that readers learn how to put these benefits to work. This section is devoted to what I refer to as the six Cs of the StoryBranding process. Following an introductory chapter where each of the six Cs are identified, the remaining chapters of Part II are devoted to each "C" separately, complete with examples of their applications, and worksheets that will allow you to put theory to work.

If Part II is like priming the walls, than Part III, Telling the Story, is about painting them. As I mentioned in the reintroduction, the main focus of this book is *not* about storytelling. Storytelling is an executional technique, while StoryBranding is a planning process. Nevertheless, in Part III, some generalized pointers tell how StoryBranding can be applied once the planning process is complete. Additionally, the last chapter discusses strategic ways to use the StoryBranding approach as a personal branding and/or personal selling tool.

Finally, Part IV consists of a collection of essays on Storybranding that have appeared on our agency's blog: blog.eswstorylab.com. These can be read at any time and are intended to supplement the main text of this book. You can also subscribe to the blog, as it is regularly updated with articles.

PART I

THE BIRTH OF A NOTION

Almost Chapter 1

If there's a book you really want to read, but it hasn't been written yet, then you must write it.
—Toni Morrison, Nobel Prize and Pulitzer Prize–winning American novelist, editor, and professor

My editor suggested I call this the "introduction." If you're like me, you like reading book introductions as much as you like sitting through fifteen minutes of movie previews or listening to the waiter drone on about the fish specials when you've already decided on the porterhouse. Okay, in truth, what follows does have the requisite *what-possessed-me-to-write-this-book* prelude for those who are curious. But it also has the *you-have-to-read-this-first-to-understand-what-follows* quality of a first chapter. So I decided to call it what it is: a half-chapter.

I went back and forth with my editor on this. But when he argued, "There's no such thing as a half-chapter," that's all I needed to confirm that I should label it "Chapter 0.5." I've always had a proclivity for breaking rules. I'm not quite sure why. As a kid, I can remember hating to be told to color within the lines or to write my "S" exactly like the one the teacher had written on the chalkboard. Fortunately, my livelihood has never depended upon how well I push a crayon. As for my handwriting, many people still mistake my signature for Jim Lignorelli.

I wasn't too concerned with the consequences back then. Today, however, I own a business and have a family, a mortgage, and retirement dreams that could fill a book twice this size. It's funny how responsibility somehow forges an appreciation for rules, sometimes even rules that don't make sense. Though I'll never lose my maverick streak, I have gotten a little better at assessing its ROI.

In keeping with my tendencies, this book breaks a few rules—more, I hope, than it prescribes. These rules are what were handed down to us in the marketing communications business as tradition. And we've followed them for a long time, perhaps blindly. My motive for writing this book isn't to start a revolt, however. It's to recognize a more powerful and creative way to define and sell a brand's unique value.

THE POWER OF STORY

As you'll see and quite by accident, we discovered the power of story, both in terms of those we tell ourselves and the ones we tell others. This discovery opened our eyes to the fact that stories have been, and still are, one of the most useful tools in our communications arsenal. Why? Well, there are many reasons, but the best among them is the purpose of story. Stories clothe truths by not getting in the way of truth. They stimulate and resonate with audiences by inviting them to identify with certain values and beliefs. Furthermore, they do this through the action of characters in response to events, and without any explication by the author.

Certainly all stories intend to sell us something. Whether it's to demonstrate the importance of love, courage, or freedom, some human value always underlies the reason stories are told. But the beauty of stories is that they reveal truth; they don't hit us over the head with it.

Brands have purpose, too. But often that purpose is too raw, too blatant, and too often driven solely by the profit motive. If we look beyond the need for immediate sales, we start to see something far more appealing than a data dump supporting rational claims about a product that allegedly make it the best, strongest, most durable, cheapest, etc. We start to see a belief, philosophy, or cause that builds super-charged associations with what the brand stands for. Instead of telling people what to think, we start giving them something to think about. Much as we form an emotional bond with story characters, we start to relate to a brand in the same way. In this way, a brand's importance goes beyond any functional advantage.

When we buy a brand, in a sense we join its tribe. In turn, we invite the brand and what it represents into our lives, and to help tell our stories to others. Brands as stories help reinforce our own self-images too. Admittedly, this is a difficult concept to get when we've been trained to believe that advertising should creatively promote advantages and benefits. Certainly advantages and benefits are important. But we are humans first, consumers second. Certainly we want things that help us to do more and/or to do it better, faster, or for less money. But above all, we are constantly striving for meaning. Brands perceived as stories to be told have a better chance of helping us find meaning than they do as things to be sold. But to tell a brand's story authentically, we have to know it first. We have to see, hear, and feel its reality because it's there, not just because consumers tell us they want it there.

THE STORYBRANDING PROCESS

StoryBranding is a process designed to help us know brands the way stories help us know ourselves. It's a process that also helps us know a brand's prospects in ways that will foster lasting relationships, immune from any competitive claim or coupon.

There's no magic trick to the StoryBranding Process. You don't have to learn any four-syllable words or embrace any ivory-tower theories. It's intuitive and easily digested. It has been proven countless times to help solve marketing communications problems with solutions that more powerfully resonate shared meaning with audiences. We easily understand it because, without being fully aware, we already use it in our everyday communications. As its name implies, StoryBranding is rooted in the logic of stories, something psychologists have shown is part of our hardwiring. With awareness, we just rely on it more effectively.

We learned about this process from principles that storytellers have been using since the beginning of language to reveal fundamental truths. And upon further investigation, we found ourselves borrowing techniques from successful brands that have, maybe unknowingly, relied upon its principles.

Some may find what follows blasphemous, as it takes on a few age-old marketing myths many of us have been saddled with since the so-called disciplines of marketing were invented. We didn't discover the Universal Truth to how advertising should be created. We did, however, find a proven way that works.

CHAPTER 1

The Inspiration

When in doubt, don't.
—*Benjamin Franklin*

My name is Jim. I am a suit.

The use of the word *suit* as an epithet has a long history. I understand that it started in England during the Victorian era and was used to describe the elite ruling class. *Suit* gained popularity here in the late 60s and early 70s as a way for the liberal youth to describe people who made up The Establishment—conservative, "my country, right or wrong" Americans in white shirts, black ties, and Nixon/Agnew stickers affixed to the chrome bumpers of their large cars. And somewhere along the line, "He's a suit" also became the way to describe anyone who worked in an advertising agency's account management department (otherwise known as "those account people").

When I arrived on the agency scene, fresh out of college with a blank slate on which I expected to enthusiastically add a long series of accomplishments, I was taken aback when people called me a suit. But

I had been raised a Catholic, so I was familiar with original sin. It's a guilty-before-proven-innocent kind of thing, and you have to be baptized in order to be cleansed of it.

So if they wanted baptism, I was going for the full-body dunk. I did everything I could to rid myself of the suit label. I started using words such as *man* (with the dragged-out a), *like*, and *far out* in my everyday speech to make people wonder if I was a stoner. My appearance was half preppy, half proletariat. Sure, I had to wear a suit, but my ties looked like Walt Disney sneezed on them in living Technicolor. I grew my sideburns down to my chin. I sported the same tinted glasses that Peter Fonda wore in *Easy Rider*. But nothing worked.

Soon, however, I learned not to take it personally.

Creatives, or people in charge of writing and producing the advertising, believed that all account people were just born to piss them off. We were regarded as vacuous, left-brained brown-nosers who were more concerned about pleasing the client than protecting the integrity of the creative product.

Over the years, advertising agency dress codes have changed. Wearing suits is pretty rare for account people these days. When they do wear suits, it's a dead giveaway that they're interviewing for another job. The really obsequious among us will wear a polo shirt with the client's logo prominently displayed for all to see, but the way most account people dress is indistinguishable from how the creatives dress. Still, the negative associations with *suit* are more than clothes-deep. To this day, many creatives think that account people wouldn't know good advertising if it grabbed them by the hand and walked them to the cash register.

At our agency, we have a rule that a good idea is a good idea, no matter who comes up with it. Although this rule encourages cooperation between creatives and account people, there are no guarantees. The wounds from wars that took place long before our agency existed run pretty deep. That said, something happened at our agency to silence the traditional account vs. creative battles. For the most part, the two sides tend to get along and respect—even like—each other. There are a lot of reasons for this, some of which could be the subject of other books. But the most important one came about as the result of understanding the root of the conflict.

In most agencies the account person is responsible for preparing a creative brief. It also goes by other names, such as *input document* or *assignment sheet*. Whatever it's called, it serves as the one-page summary of the creative assignment. It includes the basic background information that the writers and art directors (the creative team) will need to develop the advertising, including, among other particulars, a definition of the target prospect, the advertising's promise, and its desired effect. The account person's job is to fill out the creative brief, get it okayed by the boss, then present it to the client for approval. This briefing process can be brutal. On occasion, I have found myself spending hours huddled over the form debating minutiae with a client: whether *but* sounds too negative and should be replaced by *and*; the use of *from* versus *to*; and the age-old argument about the definition of an objective vs. a strategy.

It doesn't matter that the final brief might be no more inspiring than a blank piece of paper. Rather, priority is given to receiving that all-important client *green light* to start the creative process. Once the brief is blessed by the client, the account person always has the six-word key to turn off all complaints from the creative team: "This is what the client wants," often preceded by "Sorry, I've been down that road with them," or "I put my ass on the line arguing the same points," and/or "I know the client is being stubborn, but . . ." This goes on ad nauseam.

I've always been at odds with the briefing process. On one hand, it seems necessary. Clearly, writers and art directors need structure and direction. But at the same time, this practice has always seemed like an overly mechanical way to inspire originality. Consequently, creative briefs can inhibit the very thing they are designed to facilitate. In an effort to control exactly what information an ad will convey, too many planners make it hard for creativity to flourish. Additionally, creative briefs are sometimes the product of too much thinking and not enough feeling. By design, the brief is structured to require logical answers to questions that explain why the advertising is being created and what it should accomplish. Often, however, the brief will identify or label the way prospects currently feel and/or how we want them to feel about the brand being promoted. But meanings associated with feeling words are very difficult for writers, art directors, or anyone working with the brief to identify with the prospect.

If I tell you that I'm getting tired of typing right now and I need a pick-me-up, the word *tired* can mean anything from starting to fall asleep, to boredom, to being strained, exhausted, weary, drained—or it could simply mean that I'm a little less energetic than I'd like to be. Unless I do more than label the feeling *tired* by exacting a more complete picture of what tired feels like for me right now, you will never be able to reach a deeper level of empathy. Traditional creative briefs provide structure, but within that structure it is hard to discern the emotional texture needed to fuel an understanding of the prospect's problem.

In 1863, Abraham Lincoln was given a last-minute invitation to "make some appropriate comments" at the dedication of the new Soldiers' National Cemetery in Gettysburg, Pennsylvania. Imagine, if you will, that you were given the assignment of writing that speech for Mr. Lincoln. To help, you were given the creative brief on the next page.

Arguably this brief sets up goals worth achieving. But obviously, given the nature of Lincoln's Gettysburg Address, its abstract tone and dedicatory manner were derived from something much bigger than a factual checklist of what he had to say. This speech was written from Lincoln's soul as much as it was from his head. It was his heartfelt understanding of the atrocities of war that inspired the words he chose to

CREATIVE BRIEF:
GETTYSBURG ADDRESS

What is the problem this speech must solve?
Boost the Union's war effort and solidify
political support in Pennsylvania.

Target audience:
Fifteen- to twenty-thousand Northerners gathered at the
dedication of the new Soldiers' National Cemetery in
Gettysburg, Pennsylvania, and the nation at large.

What do we want them to think?
These soldiers did not die in vain.

Support:
They died to keep our government intact.

How do we want them to feel?
Respectful of the men who died in the Gettysburg battle.
Assured that we're doing the right thing.

What do we want them to do?
Continue supporting the war.

fashion this speech. Given that we're so far removed from this time in history, it'd be difficult for anyone to write anything even close to what ultimately became one of the most significant speeches ever delivered to an American audience.

But I am not suggesting that to create great advertising we have to *be* the prospect. But I am suggesting that efforts to get closer to what the prospect really thinks and feels will direct better creative output than the information-only nature of the traditional creative brief. The question is how.

As you'll soon see, we found the answer in the way stories can create empathy.

ACCIDENTAL STORYISM

A few years ago, I was summoned to visit with a client's marketing team to discuss plans for a new brand campaign for a well-known company. To protect the innocent (and myself), let's just call it the Last National Bank. I listened intently through eight hours of charts, diagrams, research summaries, and shifted paradigms. My job was to sift through all this information to find the unique selling proposition, or USP, and articulate it in a creative brief. At the conclusion of the meeting, the client asked if they could see the start of a creative brief the next morning. I saw this merely as a test to see if we were listening. Since I had been writing the brief in my head all day and merely needed to play back words on paper, I responded with a confident "yes," without hesitation.

The next morning, as I sat in my hotel room over coffee and the dreaded thought of another eight hours of death by PowerPoint, I started filling out the brief. As I was writing, I caught myself asking questions like, "Will they prefer this word over that?" or "I wonder if they'll be tripped up by the way I paraphrased their diagram," etc. As I was tying myself up in rhetorical knots, the phone rang. It was my colleague asking how long it would be before we could show them their brief. It was in that moment that everything changed.

"Let me call you right back," I said.

I suddenly realized what I was doing and why; perhaps I deserved that "suit" epithet. *Their* brief. I was writing *their* brief, as I had so many times before, simply to win *their* approval: to assuage the client's concerns and let them know that "we get it." Not once while writing did I ask myself if my words would trigger creativity, inspire new thinking, or truly help the creative team understand the prospective buyer's problem. For instance, this brief was asking for facts about the prospect, such as demographics, psychographics, ranked importance of features—things that could be assigned a number. And if anything was said about the emotional state of the prospect, the description had to be stated as an explanation of how the prospect might be feeling (e.g., "the prospect is psychologically distressed, despondent, and feeling a certain level of anxiety over his lack of control"). Beyond this was very little that would help anyone know what it was like to *be* this prospect or to help anyone empathize with his or her perspective.

I called my colleague back and said, "Give me an hour."

I quickly finished the brief as directed. But then I tried something unorthodox to see what would happen.

Instead of using descriptive language, I wrote a short letter, delivered in the first person as if I were the prospect. As such, I described who I was and the problem I was having that needed a solution. While writing it, I became like a novelist writing a mini-story that would help readers identify with the prospect. In the end I had translated the brief into something that had more of an emotional core—something that enabled the reader to vicariously feel the way the prospect feels.

An hour later, I took both the brief and the letter to the client.

Sitting across from them at a large table, I ticked off the questions and answers in the brief and received a round of approving statements from the group. Having made it over that hurdle, I then passed out the new document I had written.

"I have something else that I want to share with you," I said, to the surprise of the rest of my team. I told the client I wasn't happy with the way I had described the prospect in the creative brief. I further told them that they needed something more than a USP.

"Huh?"

"In order to create advertising that will resonate with your prospects, I think we have to do a better job of empathizing with them," I said.

As everyone looked at me quizzically (actually, *sneeringly* is a better way to describe it), I was given the green light to read what I had written:

> Hi, I AM your prospect. Ever since I've had enough money to need a bank, I've been listening to banks tell me about how much they care, how friendly they are, and how their customers are really, really happy. And I always have the same reaction: Do you actually expect me to believe that? And who cares? I sometimes wonder if there's a bank out there that knows who I am and what's most important to me.
>
> Don't get me wrong. I don't expect the red carpet to be rolled out when I come into the bank. That's not what I mean by knowing me.
>
> Knowing me is knowing that I expect my bank to get the basics done right. Like an easy-to-read, accurate statement. Like not being put on hold for fifteen minutes when I call in with a question. Like not penalizing me for using an ATM instead of a teller. Those are just some of the basics, the cost of doing business. And if that's all a bank is doing, then it needs to try a little harder.

Knowing me—I mean really knowing me—is understanding just how busy I am. Show me, don't tell me that you realize this. Somehow, let me know that you know I have a demanding job, a family, and a relentless to-do list and a number of other pressures I have to deal with regularly.

Knowing me is knowing that banking is not one of my biggest priorities in life. I don't have the time for a bank that is going to slow me down, so give me some new ideas that will make banking less of a chore. In fact, give me some ideas that will make my entire financial life less of a chore.

And hear this: I don't care how big you are. I don't care how friendly you think you are. And I certainly don't care that you never sleep or that together we can make all my dreams come true.

The solution? It's simple. In fact, that's exactly what it is. MAKE BANKING SIMPLER. Stay open late once in a while, or, at the very least, don't close the same time I leave work. Don't charge me for using an ATM. After all, you never used to charge me for using a teller. Send me statements I can understand without an MBA in finance. Don't take up my time keeping me on hold and forcing me to listen to one of your commercials, either. Stuff like that.

Oh, and one more thing: Don't just tell me you can make my life simpler. Prove it.

When I finished, you could have heard a pin drop. Eyes darted about. I thought someone might want to throw furniture at me or toss me out of the room. After a long and very pregnant pause, the president said, "Yeah, I hear things like this all the time." And that provided the permission everyone else needed before chiming in with comments like, "I've been there myself," and "That's exactly how I feel about my electric company." Everyone was adding their own experiences to the story, building layers and enriching it with meaning. Suddenly the creative brief—that cold, heartless, analytical document—had gained a pulse.

"Where did you get this idea?" the client asked.

"From you," I fibbed. (Because, honestly, I didn't know where I got the idea. It was simply born out of my own frustration that the creative brief wasn't getting me where I needed to go.) "Isn't this what all the research said?"

"Well, yes, but it's not quite the same," came the response.

"That's precisely my point. We know what the facts are. But from the brief I wrote, the one you said was on target, did you get the same feeling?"

"Well, no, of course not, but . . ."

I kept going. "Imagine a customer walking into this room. Do you think that customer would quickly summarize how they think and feel about banking in one or two sentences? You'd hear some emotion and words we'd never put on a chart or graph. In order to connect with these people, we not only have to know what they think and feel, we also have to somehow experience what they're experiencing. We have to be able to empathize with their reality."

"Well, this is all an interesting exercise, Jim," the president said, "but what are you going to do with this? Is it actionable?"

"It's a helluva lot more actionable than this creative brief," I guessed. (Because, really, I didn't know for sure until we tried it out. But I had a strong feeling about it.) "Let me take it back to the team. We'll see you in a week."

When I got back to the agency, I called a meeting. I took everyone through the same presentation that I had given the client. And the response was immediate. Suddenly the team started connecting to the prospect. They began to deeply understand the banking customers' challenges and frustrations. Unlike what they normally took from a creative brief, this was information they could process in their gut as well as in their heads.

A week later I saw some of the most engaging creative work I had ever seen for this client.

Our team went in and showed the client how we could talk about Last National Bank in a way that would truly resonate with the kinds of people I had described in the story. The advertising didn't make empty promises about a unique selling proposition that wasn't actually unique. It didn't brag. It wasn't flowery. It didn't try too hard. Rather, it was advertising that demonstrated that this bank understood "busy." And it proved it knew the importance of simplicity.

We presented this theme: *Simplify*.

That was it. In one word, we captured the essence of what this bank was all about. It described the bank's cause. We didn't come right out and say that Last National Bank made things simple. We relied instead on inference and association with the value of simplicity. This, we told our client, would become LNB's rallying cry—not just for customers who shared that value but for employees who needed to supply the proof. It's your story, we said. It's what you're all about. And it just so happens to be a story that your prospect wants and needs to hear—especially now, in these trying times.

The campaign was met with applause, which, for this client, was a first.

I knew we were onto something with this new "story" approach. Instinctively, it made sense. But exactly why and how it worked was something I couldn't yet articulate. I needed to know more to really apply it—before we could completely abandon the creative briefing process and make this a regular part of what we did. I knew there would be a ton of questions that I would have to answer.

What I eventually found was something far more powerful than a new way to write a creative brief. A new approach to creative brief writing was merely one component of something much bigger. Digging deeper, I found a whole planning method that had just been waiting to be discovered since my earliest days in the business. I can't lay claim to inventing this problem-solving process. It's been around for a very, very long time. It's one we use every day in the way we think, explain, or try to persuade others. Studies have now shown that this process is part of our hardwiring. It's a process that has its roots in story structure. And so, we call this process StoryBranding.

Review

- Clearly, writers and art directors need structure and direction. Traditional creative briefs provide structure, but within that structure it is hard to discern the emotional texture needed to fuel an understanding of the prospect's problem.

- Efforts to get closer to what the prospect really thinks and feels will direct better creative output than the information-only nature of the traditional creative brief

- Studies have shown the foundation for that what we describe as StoryBranding is a problem-solving process that is already part of our brain's hardwiring.

CHAPTER 2

Why Stories?

I felt the need to tell stories in order to understand myself.
—*Manuel Puig, Argentine author*

My experience with the Last National Bank ignited my curiosity. Intuitively I knew what I proposed would work. But I needed more clarity, more definitive reasons why. And thus, I started to dig into the subject of stories, how they work, and how we as marketers might be able to take fuller advantage of their apparent powers.

When I started my search, I was surprised to find that the subject of stories was a timely and popular topic. Recent blogs, articles, and websites about story principles were all over the Internet. Entire shelves in bookstores were stocked with newly minted books about stories.

But why now? I wondered. Stories have been a mainstay of mankind since the beginning of language. Cavemen used stories to explain how that big woolly mammoth got away. It's a safe bet that every second of every day, somebody somewhere is telling a story. So why now is there this rapidly growing newfound appreciation of stories? It's a little like calling attention to walking, talking, or other activities that we engage in habitually.

Daniel H. Pink, the author of a number of books about our changing world of work, including *A Whole New Mind: Why Right-Brainers Will Rule the Future,* provides a likely explanation for this phenomenon. In his book he states that "the era of 'left brain' dominance, and the Information Age that it engendered, are giving way to a new world in which 'right brain' qualities—inventiveness, empathy, and meaning—predominate." Pink points out that we now have machines that do our left-brain bidding. And for this reason, right-brain skills will become increasingly more valued in the workplace. One of those skills, he says, is storytelling. Pink further suggests that storytelling will become one of the most essential skills required to excel in the twenty-first century.

Thirty years ago, a similar phenomenon was predicted by John Naisbitt in his bestseller, *Megatrends.* At the time it was written, Naisbitt forecast a growing dependence on technology. And because of this, he predicted that *high tech* would need a *high touch* counterbalance. We see examples every day of just how right Naisbitt was. In fact, the term "user friendly" has become an important part of our lexicon and one often used in reference to technology.

Ironically, in the case of stories, high tech is contributing to its own counterbalance. Technology is providing us with a great number of high-touch storytelling channels. Social networks like YouTube, Facebook, and Twitter are, in effect, storytelling portals. Questions such as "What's on your mind?" or "What's happening?" provide open invitations for users to tell stories about their lives. Personal blogs have become a popular vehicle through which we can share our stories with the rest of the world. Websites such as Flickr and Picasa allow us to tell our stories through pictures. And text messaging, as well as e-mail, have increased the opportunities to tell each other stories. Technology will no doubt continue to provide us with more tools to communicate through stories.

STORIES AND BRANDING

One of those books you can find among the others on the power of story is a book by Annette Simmons titled *The Story Factor: Inspiration, Influence, and Persuasion Through the Art of Storyselling*. This book, besides adding to the explanation of story's newfound importance, contributed a quote that I now have framed over my desk. It simply reads: "Clothing truth in stories is a powerful way to get people to open the doors of their minds to the truth you carry."

This quote explains one of the most important purposes of stories: To clothe truth in order to make your truth real for others. Stories don't point a finger at us while telling us how to think and feel. Rather, they invite us to think and feel for ourselves. This helps to explain why my approach to Last National Bank worked so well. Recall that I was asked to tell management how their bank's prospects think and feel and to do this using a traditional creative brief. But instead of pointing out the facts in a one- or two-sentence description of their target prospects, I represented the prospect in a way that invited the bank's leaders to see for themselves who their prospect was.

A number of successful brands draw on this "clothing truth" principle that Annette Simmons refers to. Successful brands like Harley-Davidson, Disney, and North Face, just to name a few, don't rely solely on facts they want us to know about their products. They place a great deal of emphasis on "clothing their truth." Specifically, they promote their product claims by wrapping them in the "clothing" of the bigger causes they support, life causes their audience can identify with. In the case of Harley, the cause is living liberated. For Disney it's about the joy of magic. And for North Face, the cause is the importance of exploration. As a result, and to the extent we identify with their causes, we are more welcoming of anything they have to say relative to the typical brags and boasts we are often exposed to by advertisers.

One of the functions of the StoryBranding process is to set up the conditions for all brands to do the same. When we choose a particular brand of car to drive, a brand of beer to drink, or even a brand of toothpaste to use, we do so, in part, because of promised functional benefits. But the brands that win our loyalty and affinity are the ones that have clothed themselves in truths we share.

All brands have the potential to do more than solve functional problems. And if we think of our brand as a story, we go beyond looking for ways to find buyers. We start looking for ways to find believers. Believers are the ones that choose to evangelize brands on T-shirts, bumper stickers, or something as permanent as a tattoo. Certainly I wouldn't wear a baseball cap promoting my relationship with Charmin. But even something as personal as my choice of toilet paper can reinforce my self-identity.

STORYBRANDING VS. STORYTELLING

As I write this book, there is currently a great deal of buzz, particularly within advertising and marketing circles, about storytelling or converting advertising messages into stories. I need to emphasize that StoryBranding is not the same thing as storytelling. StoryBranding is a strategic process based on the belief that story structure, or how stories are formed, will enhance a brand's appeal. To use StoryBranding is to become more like an author with an important message and less like a salesperson with a sales quota.

Whereas the creative technique of storytelling can be a very powerful messaging device, it is not always practical to use it, given the constraints of certain media. It can be difficult, if not impossible, to fit the beginning, middle, and end of a good story on a seven-word bill-board or within a fifteen-second commercial. Instead, StoryBranding encourages one to think of a brand as a story while using tools that are similar to the ones an author would use before constructing his opening paragraph. It is about getting to the best definition of what the brand story should be about, before it is told. Thus, you won't find tips on how to decide between a first-person or third-person point-of-view. Nor will this book discuss the use of flashbacks, or how to build suspense or create irony. These subjects you can read about in texts on story technique. Nevertheless, using the StoryBranding process will put you in a very good place when it comes to choosing the most appropriate creative technique, whether it be to tell a story, provide a demonstration, use visual metaphors, or any other communications device.

StoryBranding utilizes the way stories are and have always been constructed and applies this knowledge to the brand communications process. As stated earlier, it is a planning process that urges you to think of your brand as a story with well-developed characters, plots, and themes. By doing so, you will be provided a tried-and-true way to organize and simplify your thinking. It will help you to gain a better perspective on what you are really trying to accomplish by replacing vagaries with clarity. It will help you to more effectively communicate to others what you need to accomplish. You'll be far better understood. And with greater comprehension, everyone associated with your brand will more capably enhance its effectiveness.

To think of your brand as a story, you must first become clear about what a story is. This, as I found, is not as simple as it sounds. We see, hear, and tell stories every day. We all know what a story is, right? But, as you'll see, choosing between the different definitions of what a story really is presents both problems and opportunities from a marketing perspective.

Review

- Stories have been a mainstay of communication since the beginning of language. Storytelling and other right-brain skills are becoming more important as technology takes over many of our left-brain skills.

- Stories don't point a finger at us while telling us how to think and feel. Rather, they invite us to think and feel for ourselves.

- StoryBranding draws on age-old principles of story structure to learn how we can better clothe brands with important truths or life causes.

- Successful brands promote their product claims by wrapping them in the "clothing" of the bigger causes they support, life causes their audience can identify with.

- All brands have the potential to do more than solve functional problems.

- If we think of our brand as a story, we go beyond looking for ways to find buyers. We start looking for ways to find believers. StoryBranding is not about how to convert advertising into stories. Rather, that's what we call storytelling. StoryBranding utilizes the way stories are and have always been constructed and applies this knowledge to the brand communications process.

- StoryBranding will help organize and simplify the way you think about your brand and help you better communicate that thinking to others who have a stake in the brand's success.

CHAPTER 3

What Is a Story?

Maybe stories are just data with a soul.
—*Brene Brown*

For me this quote by Brene Brown, a researcher professor at the University of Houston, Graduate College of Social Work, captures the essence of story. It explains why stories are so much more powerful than mere facts or opinions. For brands, there is clearly a parallel. Brands, too, have a soul, or at least they should in order to stand out against competitive brands that provide similar benefits. However, one of the most difficult challenges we face as marketers of our brands is knowing how to define our brand's soul as something that is real and not just manufactured. Where do we look for it? And once found, how should this soul manifest itself? By looking more closely into the composition of a story, we can start to find answers to these questions.

To get started on this journey, we need a map. More specifically, we need a good operational definition for story, something that explains how stories are structured differently than other forms of communication, and something we can use as a model to help us think of our brand as a story.

ONCE UPON A DEFINITION SEARCH

While searching for this Holy Grail definition of story, I counted eighty-two definitions on the Internet. Some were similar, but no two were exactly alike. No doubt there are more, since eighty-two is where I hoisted the white flag of surrender.

One dictionary definition is that a story is a connected series of happenings, fictitious or nonfictitious. If that's true, then the following would qualify as a story: *John went to the store. Then he walked into the store. Then he bought something.* I can't wait for the sequel.

Many of the definitions similarly have more to do with how stories sequence information. One of the most ubiquitous definitions states that stories have a beginning, a middle, and an end. I must have had one of those at the ballpark the other day. Except they called it a hot dog.

Many of the other definitions come with a dose of brain pain: *"Stories are narratives with a plot and characters generating emotion in audiences through a poetic elaboration of symbolic meanings linked together in a harmonic flow of events that can often reinforce or reset certain cognitions."* Hurts, doesn't it?

If I buy one more book on the subject of stories, I'm going to have to take out a second mortgage to pay my Amazon bill. That said, the book that I always find near the top of a very large pile is Kendall Haven's *Story Proof: The Science Behind the Startling Power of Story*. It's the result of more than a decade of research on stories—what they are, how they work, and why they're important (the whole story, so to speak). The impetus for all this work came while Haven was conducting training workshops for NASA on the application of stories to science writing. Someone from headquarters said something like, "Using stories to do science writing? Sorry, Mr. Haven, that's not how science writing works."

Determined to prove that there was a very real and practical application to science writing, Haven embarked on a journey to prove his point.

In this delightfully easy-to-read, *über*-informative book, Haven digests his findings from more than three hundred sources on the subject of stories. Okay, it doesn't read like a suspenseful Stephen King novel, but it is entertaining in its own way as it sifts through lots of erroneous information about what stories are and aren't. And about midway through the book, after all the dust has settled around all the overly analytical, protracted, and circumlocutory definitions of story out there, Haven offers this artfully simple yet very practical thirteen-word description of story:

A narrative about a character overcoming some obstacle to achieve some important goal.

As long as we find a person, real or imagined, moving through some problem toward some goal, it's a story.

With all deference to Kendall Haven, I have one slight problem with his definition. It has to do with the idea that stories are about characters *overcoming* obstacles. Not every story has a happy ending. In fact, some of the best stories are those in which the obstacle is not overcome. Shakespeare called these tragedies to contrast them from comedies. So with that, I offer up this slight twist on Haven's definition of story. It is the fourteen-word version that we will refer to throughout this book:

A narrative about a character *dealing with an* obstacle to achieve some important goal.

With that small fix, we're good to move forward.

THE "GOOD" STORY

But what is a "good" story? Haven, being the scientist that he is, is very objective in the way he describes what stories are. Consequently, he does not offer a definition of what a *good* story is. For that we have to turn to the artists. It just so happens that those artists are us. What is good to you may not be good to me. Nevertheless, there are some general principles that we all apply when it comes to determining the difference between a good and bad story. As you'll soon see, these are important from a branding standpoint as well. Imagine someone telling you this story:

While Joe was driving to the concert, he heard the thump, thump, thump of his front tire going flat.

"Oh my God," he thought. "I have a flat tire!"

He pulled over. He fixed the tire. Lo and behold, glory hallelujah, he made it to the concert.

Although it meets all the conditions of our story definition, I think we can all agree that it hardly has the makings of a best seller. There is no significant reason the story is being told. If someone were to tell you this story, you might politely nod and smile. And it would be hard to resist the thought of "who cares?" Thus, just because a story meets the conditions of our story definition does not guarantee that it will be something of interest. We have to dig a little deeper to find what makes a story good or important.

PLOTS AND THEMES

Some of the answers to questions about what makes a good story can be ascertained by deconstructing the elements of story. Doing so will also show us important parallels between good stories and desirable brands. The first of these are plot and theme. The relevancy of these two elements to branding provides the foundation upon which the Story-Branding approach is built.

First, let's define terms:

A plot is comprised simply of the events that tell a story.

A story's theme is the message, lesson, or moral that gives a story meaning and is surmised from the story's plot.

In other words, plots describe events; themes provide meaning.

Let's take a closer look at each of these two elements and then discuss their application to branding, starting with plot.

A plot is really the logical, rational, sequential component of a story. One of its most important functions is to provide audiences with an understanding of the happenings that make up the story. Story plots can be represented by a formula.

For instance, the formula of a mystery might be: A crime has occurred and it is assumed that B or C is the culprit. Our super sleuth investigator X deduces that it is neither B nor C, but D that committed the crime. Surprise! D is the police commissioner. The End.

The formula for a love story might be something like: A is married to B. They have two a's and b's. A is a happy mother but a lonely wife. She then meets C and falls madly in love. After a long internal struggle, she decides to tell B about her paramour. B kills everyone, including himself. The End. (I'm just a sucker for happy endings.)

The point is that plots are logical. No matter what happens during a story, in the end, problems are solved, and answers to questions that come up are provided or we are left to arrive at them ourselves. In the end, though, we have a need to make sense of plots; otherwise we are left unsatisfied.

Themes, on the other hand, are the story's *why*, or the author's purpose for telling the story beyond selling books or movie scripts. Sometimes referred to as the lesson, the message, or the moral of the story, themes convey the author's truth about human nature.

As children, we were introduced to simple themes through fables and fantasies, themes like "don't be greedy" or "work should come before play." Themes are sometimes plainly stated at the end of a story or are left for us to debate among ourselves. But in all cases, only we can decide if the theme has relevancy for us.

Our response to plots is usually driven by our need to reduce uncertainty or a need to know how things work out. The logical side of our brain processes plots. In contrast, our response to themes is often quite visceral, as it can be driven by deeply held feelings below the threshold of consciousness. In any case, themes are subjective. Whether or not we go along with the theme of a story is dependent upon how well it can fit within our own belief structures. And depending on how well it fits (or doesn't fit) within our own belief structure, we may find ourselves becoming emotionally involved with it. I once saw a movie that made a strong statement about child abuse and how prevalent it is. For many days later, I couldn't shake off the impact this had on me.

Perhaps you can readily see the parallels between stories and brands given this discussion of plots and themes. If not, consider that plots are very much like the products that are branded, and themes can have a lot to do with the brand itself.

Let's see how.

PLOTS AND PRODUCTS

Plots, like products, must provide some worthwhile experience in order to justify an audience's expenditure of time and money. Both plots and products rely on reported facts (or the pretense of facts, in the case of fiction) supplied by their creators. However, as interesting as a plot or product might be, neither conveys much meaning beyond their functional purpose.

Take, for instance, the typical James Bond movie. As much as we may enjoy it, its significance doesn't go beyond suspense, special effects, and the ability of one man to attract some of the most beautiful women in the world. The function of a typical James Bond movie is to provide little more than a fantasy escape. That's okay; sometimes that's all we want from a story. But James Bond movies are rarely the ones that get nominated for Best Picture awards. Instead, the movies that do are the ones that have special significance beyond their plots and production values. They provide added value by providing more than just a nice ride or a laugh. They convey meaning. They inspire, empower, and/or teach us something. They provide a powerful message that the author believes we need to know and appreciate.

Products are designed to solve problems and/or present opportunities similar to the way plots show how problems are solved by a character or characters. But why will people pay more for branded products than generics? Why will people spend $150 for a pen when they can buy a Bic for 29 cents? Understanding brand themes provides some answers.

THEMES AND BRANDS

Brands can provide the emotional connection that plots and products need in order to engage their respective audiences. Notice I used the word "can." This is because sometimes brands, like in the James Bond example I gave earlier, provide little emotional connection. Given this weak emotional connection, the brand name does little more than discriminate its products from the backdrop of its competition. The image it creates is colorless.

A brand with a well-developed theme can make its products meaningful and memorable because, in addition to some functional purpose, the brand itself can help its audience identify with important values and beliefs that are strongly adhered to and shared by other members of that audience. Just as a love story can call up meaning, a computer can do likewise by associating itself with strongly held beliefs and human values.

The challenge is for brands to do what story themes do and to emulate the way themes get communicated through stories. A primary goal of this book is to show how that challenge can be met through the StoryBranding process. There's much more to come. But let me just give you a sampling by discussing what I think is one of the most important ways brands can benefit from having something akin to a story theme. And as you'll see, for a brand to have what is often referred to as a "theme line" does not necessarily mean that it qualifies as having a story theme in the truest sense of what a story theme is and how it works. In fact, many so-called theme lines provide nothing more than a summary of their plots.

THEME THINK

"Storytelling reveals meaning without committing the error of defining it." This quote by German philosopher Hannah Arendt is one I use often to explain how brands can benefit from what I call *theme think*.

Stories move us to the extent we ascribe importance to them. Stories don't hit us over the head with expository presentations and logical arguments about the meaning the author intends for to convey. Editorials function that way more than stories. Through stories, we alone decide whether or not the story is meaningful. Convincing us to think and feel a certain way would be like the comedian telling why his joke is funny. *Theme think* is what we do when we cast the theme as meaningful without arguing in favor of its meaningfulness. This aspect of story provides innumerable lessons for brands.

We once worked for a casino client that wanted audiences to see it as the place for what they described as the "hip and cool" crowd. In an effort to promote the value of "hip and cool," they had been running ads that read, "We're happening. Are you?" Another ad was headlined "Catch the Vibe." Our first order of business was to convince this client that cool people don't tell others they are cool. In effect, their advertising was committing the error of theme think's nemesis, theme *tell*.

Instead of ads proclaiming how cool this casino was, we created advertising that relied solely on associating with the quality of "cool" rather than directly informing audiences this casino was cool. In fact, the commercials we developed were void of any copy read by a voice-over. A series of commercials merely provided aspirational slices of life told through the eye candy of special effects and titillating visuals. In effect, the ads attempted to show this casino's "vibe" rather than brag about it, leaving members of the target audience free to decide for themselves whether or not this casino held any meaning that was relevant and important. And they decided in the affirmative. This approach helped this casino achieve remarkable gains in traffic and revenue.

Brands, like story themes, are better left to interpretation than explanation. The extent to which they are explained is the extent to which they are ignored, or worse yet, discounted. In general, very few of us like to be told how to think. A line can and should be drawn between influencing value and pushing it. Once that line is crossed, brands get in their own way.

Understanding the way story themes work underscores the futility of outward statements of the value or values that marketers want associated with their brands. Yet we are consistently bombarded with explicit statements of values, typically starting with the pronoun "we" in so-called theme lines, e.g., "We care, help, know, think, believe," etc. It doesn't matter what "we" think. What matters is what our audiences think or have come to think about what our brand represents.

Legendary brands communicate meaning the way story themes do, through implication as opposed to explication. When they were introduced, phrases like "Just Do It" for Nike, "Think Different" for Apple, and "Be All That You Can Be" for the Army, in the truest sense of what a theme line is, implied rather than explained what their brands were all about.

As a side note, it's important to see that themes and brands work best when they ride the coattails of important values and beliefs we already subscribe to. In his book *All Marketers Are Liars: The Power of Telling Authentic Stories in a Low-Trust World*, Seth Godin states:

> *The best stories don't teach people anything new. Instead, the best stories agree with what the audience already believes and makes the members of the audience feel smart and secure and reminded that they were right in the first place.*

Whereas we can try to shape meaning, we can only go so far before we get in our own way. This is especially true for mature brands to consider. Some brands have meanings that have become entrenched over time. Oftentimes, in order to combat obsolescence, a brand will go to extremes trying to change its existing frame of reference. This is what Oldsmobile tried to do when it tried to convince us that it was "not our father's Oldsmobile." More recently, KFC tried to convince us to "Unthink KFC" when they introduced grilled chicken and lost business while ignoring their loyal base of fried chicken consumers. And then there's JCPenney, a brand that recently added itself to a long list of brands whose efforts to radicalize their identities backfired.

You'll read more about the theme/brand parallel, as it will come up during various discussions of how to use the StoryBranding process. But first, let's turn our attention to the StoryBranding Model on which this process is built.

Review

- Story is an oft-used word to describe a number of different types of communication.

- The working definition of a story that will be used throughout this book is "a narrative about a character dealing with an obstacle to achieve some important goal."

- The difference between a story and a *good* story is that the good story has personal relevance.

- Plots are the sequential events of a story that explain the what. Themes consist of our interpretation of a story or why. Plots and products consist of explicit information. Themes and brands are made up of interpretive information.

- Legendary brands communicate meaning the way story themes do—through implication as opposed to explication.

- The best stories agree with what the audience already believes.

- Oftentimes, in order to combat obsolescence, a brand will go to extremes trying to change its existing frame of reference. The results can be disastrous.

CHAPTER 4

The Brand Story's "Cells"

Until you can almost intuitively see the difference between story structure and storytelling in a completed story, you stand little chance of being able to employ that knowledge in creating your own stories.
—*Melanie Anne Phillips, creator of StoryWeaver software*

A while back, I decided that I didn't have enough conflict in my already time-starved life, so I took up golf. I had played a lot of baseball when I was a kid. And I've been a fairly avid tennis player most of my life. So I thought, *Okay, what could be so hard*? The golf ball is smaller, and how difficult could it be to hit a ball that doesn't move?

After a couple of rounds I realized that I was spending almost as much on lost balls as I was for greens fees. One day, after letting the third foursome play through, in the sixth hour of our 18-hole round and just as my ball ricocheted off a tree to a place twenty-five yards behind where I hit it, a friend broke down, practically in tears, and yelled, "JIM! BEFORE YOU KILL SOMEBODY, WOULD YA GET SOME LES-SONS?" Actually, he added a few other words to spice up his point, but I won't go there.

My first lesson consisted of a golf pro videotaping my swing. Using some sophisticated video computer program, the pro proceeded to show me that I had a hunched stance, an exaggerated knee bend, a weak grip, crooked alignment, poor ball placement, an overly quick backswing, no weight shift, an inside-out swing plane, a wristy release, little balance, and no follow-through, and, as if to throw in just a little more encouragement, he told me that I needed a lot of help. I decided to get a second opinion.

The second pro conducted a similar videotaping exercise, but instead of going through all the gory details, he isolated my problem into three categories: my address, my swing, and my follow-through. (Which, of course, is pretty much everything, but he sure made it sound a lot less intimidating!) He then proceeded to spend time on each one separately. Through the course of his lessons, he got to all the same problems that the first pro identified. But by concentrating everything into three categories, he left me far less overwhelmed.

It's been a while since I took those lessons, and I still lose a lot of golf balls. But I'm not quite the death threat I used to be on the course.

Storytelling, unlike golf, is relatively intuitive. Nobody told the cave dweller how to tell a story. I'm pretty sure Shakespeare didn't take lessons. Nevertheless, structuring a good story and, specifically, a good *brand* story is something that can be enhanced with a richer understanding of what story structure can reveal to us. And to share what I think are the most important concepts appropriate to brand planning, I've decided to follow the lead of my more successful golf instructor. Instead of throwing everything at you at once, I'm going to start by simply introducing the mechanics of the Storybranding Model before showing you how to put it to work.

THE STORYBRANDING MODEL

The StoryBranding Model consists of two character *cells* separated by obstacles. Similar to the way we define a story, this model also consists of a character's movement through the obstacles toward some goal—except in our model, the main character of the story is the brand itself.

The brand's goal is to create a relationship or connect with the prospect. In order to do this, two things must occur. First, the brand must interact with each of the obstacles and successfully meet the challenges that each obstacle presents. Second, and while doing this, the brand must begin to cultivate a relationship with the prospect. This relationship will grow in intensity with each successive obstacle that is overcome.

The cells are composed of outer layers or behaviors. For the brand, the outer layer consists of price, packaging, features, and functional benefits, all of which are discernible to our five senses. For the prospect, the outer layer mainly consists of desired physical behaviors or perceived problems that a given product can solve, i.e., finding a car within a certain budget, buying an over-the-counter remedy to lessen a headache, etc.

At the center of each cell is an inner layer. This consists of the inner beliefs and values that serve as the ultimate motivation for both the brand and the prospect's behaviors. This is where the brand adds psychic and emotional value to itself beyond its physical features and functional promises. For the prospect, the inner layer is what explains how one brand of product can become preferred over another that performs a similar function. The connection between the inner and outer layer is somewhat complex but will become more apparent to you as you read through the summary descriptions of each cell. Furthermore, Part II of this book is organized to explain each cell's composition more thoroughly and will show how this model can illuminate insights that might otherwise be missed.

The StoryBranding Model

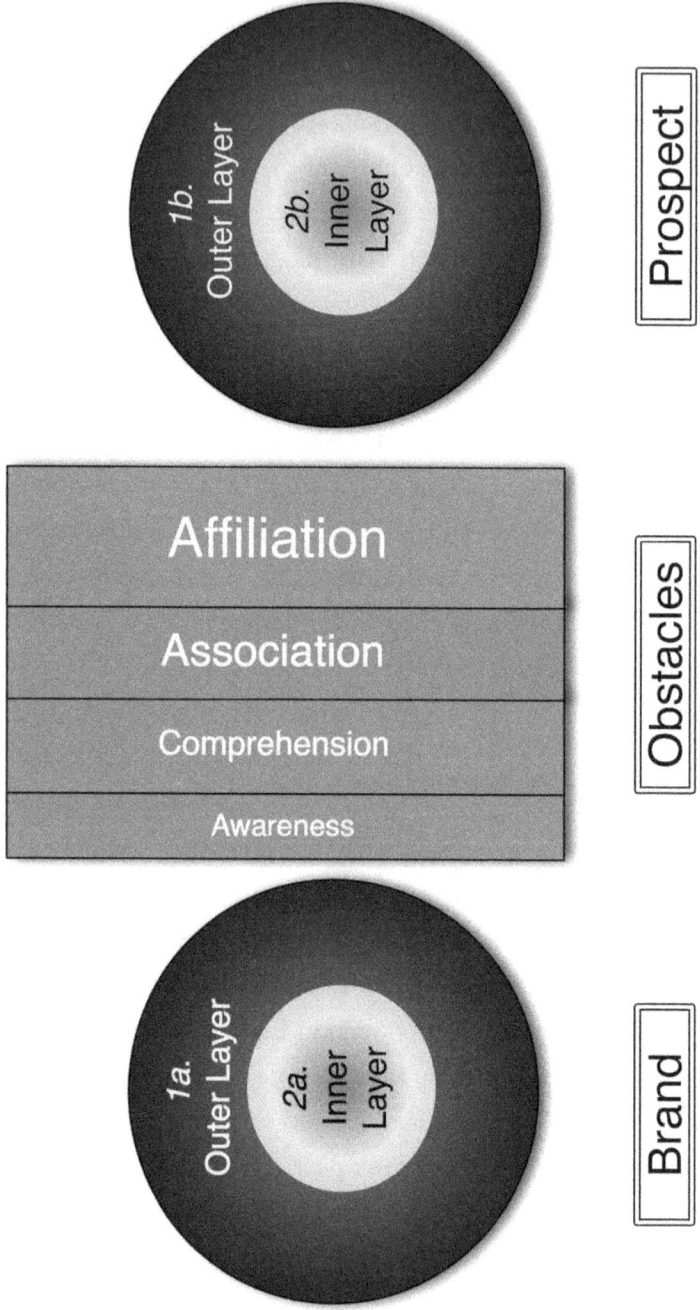

Prospect

1b. Outer Layer
2b. Inner Layer

Affiliation

Association

Comprehension

Awareness

Obstacles

1a. Outer Layer
2a. Inner Layer

Brand

The Character Cells

Any brand story has two main characters: the protagonist brand itself and its beneficiary, the prospect. The brand has set out to provide the prospect with more than just a unique product or service. It is looking to cultivate a relationship with the prospect, one that will establish loyalty and turn the prospect into a missionary for the brand. To do this, the brand must deal with certain obstacles.

The Obstacles

Often, when obstacles are discussed in marketing, they refer to sales barriers. From a story perspective, we look beyond sales and consider obstacles that prevent the buyer or seller from connecting with the brand as described earlier. As each obstacle is overcome, the connection between the brand and the prospect becomes stronger. But until all obstacles are effectively dealt with, the prospect is vulnerable to the advances of competitive brands.

Character Cell Layers

Both the brand and the prospect cells have two layers. Their outer layers consist of physical and behavioral properties of the characters. Their inner layers are composed of deeper, often hidden beliefs and values that are linked to and responsible for character behaviors.

1a: The Brand Cell's Outer Layer

The brand cell's outer layer consists of the physical design of the product and how it functions to satisfy the prospect's outer layer needs. If the brand is a service, then the deliverables of that service, which are a function of its operations, comprise its outer layer. In effect, the brand's outer layer is both perception and reality. It manifests itself in how the brand is perceived to behave in addition to how it actually behaves.

2a: The Prospect Cell's Outer Layer

The prospect cell's outer layer first consists of the prospect's measurable traits and characteristics. These often consist of traditional demographic characteristics like age, sex, income, and education, but they can also include important and relevant roles that the character assumes (e.g., parent, student, purchaser, etc.). It might also include a life stage (e.g., married with young kids, older, retired, etc.). If you are familiar with PRIZM research available through Claritas, you may recall that what is often described in one of their geodemographic clusters is material that would make up the prospect's outer layer.

But the prospect's outer layer mainly consists of a description of the relevant problem that the prospect is trying to solve. It could be a function that the prospect wants to accomplish (e.g., a car battery that will start in the coldest weather, or less manufacturing downtime). Or it could be a function that has become problematic and requires a solution different from and better than one that has been tried before.

1b: The Brand Cell's Inner Layer

The brand's inner layer is sometimes referred to as the brand's essence or its DNA. It consists of values and beliefs that the brand becomes associated with. The brand's outer layer is the church. Its inner layer is the religion that is practiced inside the church. When the brand's inner layer and the prospect's inner layer connect, potential for the strongest possible relationship ensues, much the same as when important values are shared between people.

2b: The Prospect Cell's Inner Layer

This constitutes the prospect's self and/or aspirational identity and serves as a point of inner connection with the brand. It is composed of the prospect's values and beliefs that are relevant to the brand and account for the potential strength of the brand–prospect relationship.

As you see from the description of this model, the running thread is the notion that the brand's relationship with the prospect is the all-important objective. There are a number of reasons for this, as you will see in the next chapter.

Review

- Like story structure, a brand can be seen as dealing with obstacles to achieve a relationship with its prospect.

- The StoryBranding Model consists of two character cells separated by an obstacle.

- The cells are composed of outer layers or behaviors we can see, and inner layers or values and beliefs that aren't readily discernible but explain the outer-layer behaviors.

- To connect or attach the cells to each other, we must deal with the challenges presented by each obstacle. As each obstacle is overcome, the relationship between the brand and the prospect strengthens.

- Matching occurs when there is a logical consistency between the outer layers and the inner layers of the brand and prospect cells.

CHAPTER 5

The "Good" Brand Story

*People have forgotten how to tell a story. Stories don't have a middle or an
end any more. They usually have a beginning that never stops beginning.*
—*Steven Spielberg*

In 1898, an insurance salesman by the name of E. St. Elmo Louis created
a model that you may be familiar with. For some, it still explains the goal
of marketing communications. The model goes by the acronym AIDA
(pronounced Aid-uh). It suggests that the seller must effect a sequence
of mind-states starting with *A* for awareness; *I* for interest; *D* for desire;
and *A*, again, this time for action, which should really be *P* for purchase,
but Aid-pee just doesn't have the same ring.

The final goal of marketing is always action or the purchase itself.
This goal is easy to love. It's measurable; it keeps shareholders happy,
employees gainfully employed, and chief marketing officers from having
to dust off their resumes prematurely.

However, to think that this defines the ultimate goal of brand marketing can lead to a number of problems and missed opportunities. For

instance, the AIDA model ignores the fact that the prospect can be a source of repeat sales and/or referrals long after any action takes place. A brand's best customers are often the brand's best marketers. AIDA may work for a brand that is purposefully short-lived, but there aren't too many of them.

As StoryBranders believe (I don't mean us to sound like a cult, but this designation does happen to describe how we think) and as was discussed in the previous chapter, we see the brand's primary goal as forming a strong relationship with the prospect. Moreover, we ultimately want this relationship to be strong enough to garner repeat and/or referral business through word of mouth. It follows that, as we start to achieve this relationship, sales will naturally ensue. Additionally, the stronger the relationship and the more people the brand relates to, the better the short- *and* long-term sales outcome. In addition to this, the brand might start selling itself and require fewer advertising dollars.

Like E. St. Elmo Louis's model, however, the StoryBranding Model holds that the brand must generate a chronology of mind-states within the prospect. These mind-states change during the life of the brand–prospect relationship, from the beginning when it is formed, and as it evolves into a bond that competitors can't penetrate. The relationship can potentially gain strength through time if certain obstacles are properly addressed along the way.

THE JOURNEY TOWARD A STRONG CONNECTION

From the time that the eyes of the prospect meet the brand, the brand–prospect relationship has begun to form. At first the connection is weak, but over time and through the brand's activities, the relationship can be strengthened.

As you can see from this illustration of a brand's roadmap, I have identified different stops along a brand's path, starting with its introduction. These connection points are like road signs along the way to Level IV, which is the final destination. Leading up to Level IV, the brand–prospect relationship strengthens as the brand achieves certain milestones prescribed by each signpost. The four connection points are labeled with what is most responsible for the strength (or lack of strength) in the brand–prospect relationship. They are product function awareness, product feature comprehension, brand association, and brand affiliation. At each level, the brand–prospect connection potentially grows stronger.

When I present this idea, I use my wallet as a prop to illustrate the brand's journey. I use a wallet because it is a fairly mundane object. Unlike cars, shoes, or beer, a branded wallet is not something we usually think of when we are considering brands that can achieve strong connections with prospects. A man's wallet is a wallet is a wallet. Or is it? Using a least likely suspect helps one to see how these connection points can exist for all brands, even the ordinary ones.

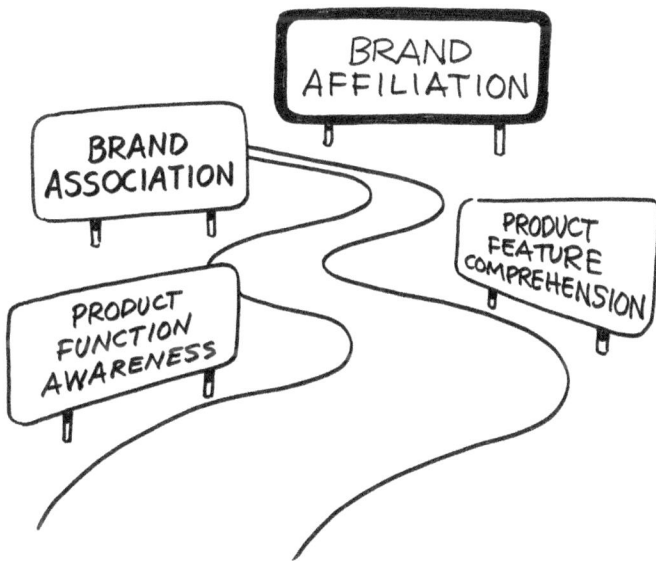

Level I: Product Function Awareness

So imagine, if you will, a man who sees a TV commercial for something called a "wallet." He has never seen anything like this before. Up until this point he had been wrapping his cash, credit cards, and IDs with a rubber band.

"Amazing! What will they think of next?" he thinks. He decides to buy one.

At this level, the prospect's connection to the brand is weak. In fact, he doesn't care what the brand name is. He may not even remember the brand name. He is primarily interested in the functional benefit that the product can deliver.

Level II: Product Feature Comprehension

The prospect has been using his wallet for a while. It is starting to get a little worn. So he visits the department store and notices that, since time has passed and wallets are catching on, he now has a number of wallets to choose from. He notices, for instance, that he can now own a wallet with twelve credit-card compartments instead of the four he has been forced to deal with. It's a different brand of wallet from the one he's been carrying around. But who cares? Those twelve credit card compartments will come in handy, and the wallet branded ACME is the only one that offers this feature. He now has a connection with the ACME brand, albeit weak. It is weak because it merely represents a product function that is unique.

Level III: Brand Association

Two years pass, and our prospect has, once again, worn out his wallet. By now, wallets have really become the rage. In fact, they now take up a whole section of the department store. Product differences start to become less dramatic. One brand of wallet may have twelve compartments while another has thirteen. Looking through all of the displays, our prospect sees a number of brand names he is familiar with. Any of these would be perfectly acceptable. But ACME, given his experience with the brand, is high within his consideration set. This is because ACME has come to mean something to him. Specifically, he associates ACME with words like "quality" and "durability." Other brands could achieve similar associations, but his familiarity with the ACME brand solidifies his associations—to the extent that he is not quite ready to switch to a different brand.

Level IV: Brand Affiliation

It is here that the strongest connections with a brand are formed. Here the meaning that the prospect associates with the brand are deeply important and are more aligned with human values or beliefs. All of a sudden our prospect starts seeing some new TV ads for ACME wallets. They show a picture of a handsome man pulling out his wallet to pay his hotel bill while standing next to a gorgeous woman. She looks over to him with adoring

eyes and flirtatiously says, "Oh, excuse me, isn't that an ACME wallet?"

"Yes, it is," he says, smiling back at her. A conversation ensues as she rubs the fine leather. "Yep, that's me," our prospect thinks. "Cool and confident; a real lady killer."

Now, every chance our prospect gets, he shows off his ACME wallet. When he attends business meetings, for instance, he takes it out of his pocket and puts it on the table for all to see. He wants everyone to know that he is that guy in the ACME ads. And for years he continues to buy ACME wallets, even though their prices have skyrocketed and other wallets on the market are just as good. In addition to existing associations our prospect had with this wallet before seeing the advertising, ACME now becomes a story that can tell the world who this prospect is and what he aspires to.

GETTING TO LEVEL IV

I've obviously taken some license to exaggerate what happens at each connection level in this example of a wallet's journey toward brand affiliation. Nevertheless, all brands, as their product categories mature, are presented with similar opportunities for these different levels of connection with their designated prospects. I use this example to point out a few things.

Each level defines a stage in the brand/consumer relationship, from acquaintance in Level I to best friend in Level IV. Contrary to what many believe is the case, the brand itself doesn't really start to develop a strong relationship that will add value to the product until it reaches Level III. Up until that point, the focus is really on becoming familiarized with the product. Granted, certain product advantages may be ascribed to one brand over another. And those advantages may, in fact, be responsible for driving a favorable purchase decision. But it is important to always keep in mind that if a prospect is simply buying because of a product advantage, the brand name is nothing more than an identifying label. As we've discussed, too often marketers equate their brands with their products. But brands and products have entirely different purposes. A product's purpose is functional. A brand's purpose is meaningful.

The Level IV connection represents the ultimate goal of brand marketing communications. It is here that the brand starts to say something about beliefs and values that the prospect can identify with or aspire to. The brand takes on a meaning beyond the product that it represents.

When the prospect has a Level I or Level II connection with a brand, the brand story is primarily all plot. The emphasis is on the product function more than on any meaning that could be associated with the brand. At Level III the brand starts to take on meaning, but the story theme is not fully resonant and empowering until the brand reaches Level IV. It is at this level of connection that the brand becomes valued as a "good" story among target prospects who share the same value. Product benefits are important, but as the brand affiliation becomes even stronger, they can become secondary in importance. As such, the brand's meaning adds importance to the product, so much so that prospects might even pay more for the brand than alternative brands that offer similar or even better benefits.

Additionally, the power of the brand's meaning will protect it from competitive inroads. Additionally, prospects once affiliated with the brand become missionaries that further enhance the brand's growth through word of mouth. Is it no surprise that the purpose of the StoryBranding process is to manage the brand so that it reaches, sustains, and builds an affiliation connection with the prospect?

OBSTACLES ALONG THE WAY

The brand's journey to achieve a Level IV connection is full of pitfalls, however. Sometimes the brand must move backward before moving forward. Competitive forces will mount assaults on comprehension of the brand's unique product benefits and/or confidence in the brand name itself. These assaults must be dealt with continuously. Certain safeguards against competitive threats are granted once a brand establishes a Level IV connection with a prospect, making this level all the more important to reach. But it is rare that a brand will quickly get to Level IV without having to deal with certain obstacles. Knowing this, the smart brand will see from day one that Level IV is worth seeking. In so doing, it will prepare for its Level IV arrival by determining ahead of time what its value is. This is so that when the brand reaches Level IV, it doesn't have to backtrack or reinvent what it stands for. It merely needs to amplify a meaning that has been there all along.

Brands that have reached Level IV include Nike, The North Face, Victoria's Secret, Disney, Southwest Airlines, and others. None of these brands just turned on their Level IV magnetism one day during their existence. As they were going through the first three levels of connection, their Level IV connection had already been envisioned and planned. Although their products received most of the attention during the first three levels of connection, visages of their desired Level IV connection could be seen in all marketing communications. Now having arrived at Level IV, these brands are able to fully concentrate on what they stand for, which, in turn, helps them all enjoy high margins and a loyal, happiness-spreading customer base.

Whereas the connections are arrived at sequentially, each connection level receives different degrees of emphasis during the brand's life cycle. Each connection level is much like a plate that must be spun before the next can be spun. But all plates must be kept spinning, even for the brands that have successfully reached Level IV.

HOW TO MEASURE THE CONNECTION

As a starting point, a brand might want to understand where it is on the connection roadmap. This can be measured simply by determining the extent to which each level has been achieved. Measures of functional awareness, feature comprehension, brand associations, and brand affiliation are stacked up next to each other on the following graph.

Here the brand has been recently introduced, as reflected by low-level or no-level scores across each of the four connection variables. Only 25 percent of the total audience is aware, and a mere 5 percent of the total audience has reached both Level I and Level II. Clearly, product function awareness and product feature comprehension have to be given priority.

On the other hand, the second chart shows that a very high percentage of the total audience has reached Levels I, II and III, whereas only 5 percent has achieved all four levels.

Clearly more emphasis should be given to building confidence and affiliation with the brand.

Too often, we see brands with charts that look something like the first one. They become stuck in a Level I and II rut. This occurs when a brand cannot get beyond awareness and comprehension for its product. When this occurs, it is often because the brand itself has become its own obstacle. You know your brand has fallen prey to this problem when adjectives used to describe it are inconsistent or contradictory. Brand meaning has become too fragmented. Your brand, standing for too many things, stands for nothing.

More often than not, the rut that exists is directly related to the fact that the brand has done very little to influence a single-minded association with some important belief or value, or it has left too much of its meaning to the whim of customers. It can also occur when the brand tries too hard to associate itself with something that the consumer finds

Cumulative Connection Achievement

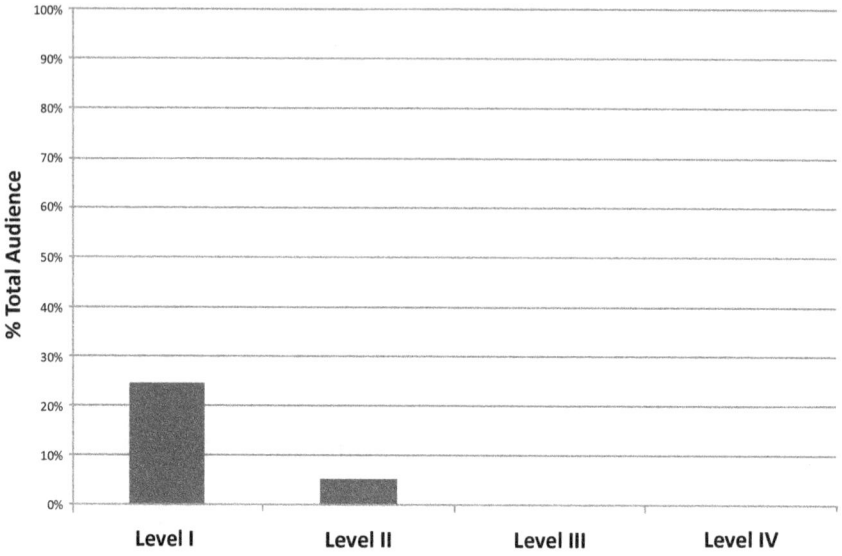

Cumulative Connection Achievement

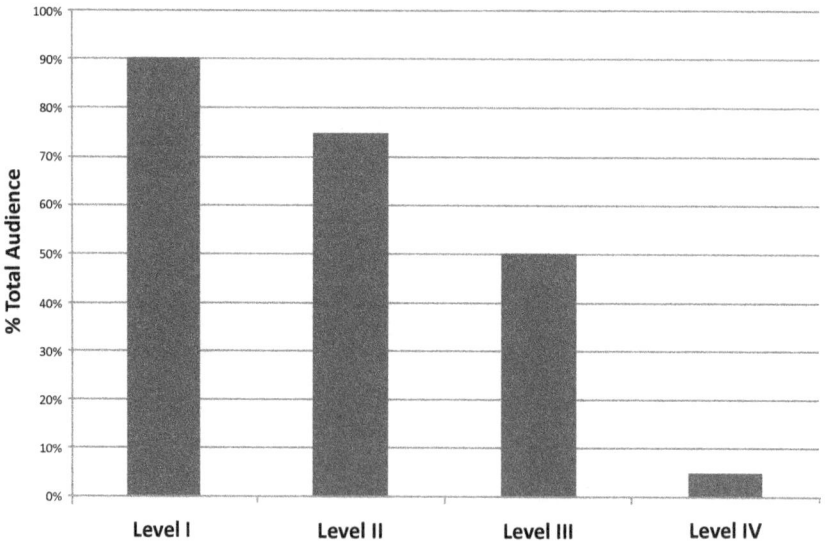

unbelievable, such as the Arby's "Good Mood Food" campaign. As such, the brand name does little or nothing to add value to the product.

If you are continually talking about features and benefits in your advertising, and without regard for the unique meaning you want associated with your brand, you are probably falling victim to this problem. As such, your brand is becoming vulnerable to competition. Keep in mind that it's easy for competitors to copy features and benefits that are the focus of Level I and II. However, it is very difficult to copy an exclusive meaning, which is the focus of Level III. The difference between Level III and Level IV is the difference in importance of the meaning associated with your brand. Level III has to be dealt with before even thinking about Level IV. Brand associations can't become important if they don't exist.

Where the Level I and II rut occurs most is in cases where the brand being sold is a person. This person could be a job applicant, speaker, blogger, lawyer, doctor, tax consultant, etc. Remember that if you have a birth certificate, you are a brand. Any audience you are appealing to must be able to relate to what you're all about and beyond the facts of your resume or what you tell others about what you do. Many people have a background similar, or even stronger, than yours. If you have any doubts, look up your job title on LinkedIn and compare what you are saying about yourself to what others are saying about themselves. If it's similar, it's time you translate your experience into a unique value or belief that you stand for and fully support through your actions. You need to move through Level II and Level IV obstacles. This comes under the heading of personal StoryBranding, a subject we'll tackle toward the end of the book. But don't go there yet. You'll first need a better understanding of the StoryBranding process and how to put it to work. And that is what we'll cover in Part II.

Review

- The belief that sales achievement defines the ultimate goal of brand marketing can lead to a number of problems and missed opportunities.

- The primary goal for the brand should be to achieve a strong relationship with the prospect. Sales will follow.

- A strong relationship with the prospect will also help to achieve referral business through word of mouth.

- The brand's journey toward a strong relationship with the prospect consists of four levels:

- Level I: Product Function Awareness

- Level II: Product Feature Comprehension

- Level III: Brand Association

- Level IV: Brand Affiliation

- Although the connection levels are arrived at sequentially, each connection level receives different degrees of emphasis during the brand's life cycle.

- Until the brand is able to achieve a Level III connection with the prospect, the connection is more product dependent than brand dependent.

- Level IV, or Brand Affiliation, represents the ultimate goal for any brand. The brand's journey toward a Level IV connection is full of pitfalls, sometimes requiring a move backward before moving forward.

- Measuring the extent to which each level has been achieved can help determine what has yet to be accomplished.

PART II

STORYBRANDING

CHAPTER 6

The StoryBranding Process

Tell a joke that lacks classic story structure, and see if anyone laughs.
—Adam Sexton, The Writer's Store

I grew up in Detroit, Michigan. Telling people that Detroit at the time was the fourth-largest city in the United States usually prompts a snide comment or two about how old I must be to have lived there so long ago. Actually, it *was* long ago. And it's true that because of hard times Detroit has dramatically shrunk in size. Nevertheless, Detroiters among us will take pride in the fact that Detroit is a city that typifies team-work. In Detroit, anyone and everyone affiliated with the auto industry is somehow, some way connected to everyone else who has something to do with making and selling the automobile.

One of my first jobs as a high school student was as a sweeper for a plant that manufactured piston rods. My job was to clean up the metal chips on or around the lathes. It wasn't the sexiest job, but it was impor-tant. Stray chips that could find their way into the lathes would cause the malfunctioning of equipment, resulting in factory downtime.

Finished piston rods would be sent to another factory, where they would be fit into piston housings. The piston housings would then be shipped to a place where they would be assembled into engines. The engines would be shipped to the car company's assembly plant, where they would be joined with other parts manufactured at other outlets throughout the city. Every person in every job associated with designing, manufacturing, and marketing their products (including sweepers) was highly dependent upon every other. Consequently, the vast majority of Detroit's citizenry were, and still are, brethren in one of the most important outputs of this country: the automobile. Teamwork and interdependence are values I always associate with Detroit. In effect, I have, and probably always will have, a Level IV connection with Detroit as a brand of city, despite its troubles.

The StoryBranding process is analogous to the way cars are made. It is, in effect, the assembly line for component parts of the brand story. And when the final product rolls off this assembly line, its success or failure is highly dependent on how well the parts combine to create the basis for any brand story. In this section of the book, you're going to be taken on a guided tour of the StoryBranding assembly line. This tour is designed to help you both explore and address the facets of your brand that will ultimately affect its story.

THE STORYBRANDING PROCESS

What follows describes the six Cs of the StoryBranding process. If you'd like to print it out, an easy reference guide is found on pages 70 and 71. It shows the workflow from one task to the next, right up through the creation of a StoryBrief. Completing this entire process will help you arrive at a marketing-communications plan that will serve as the blueprint for all brand communications, both externally and internally. The completed StoryBrief will set the stage for the execution of communications in any form and across any medium as your brand mounts an attack on identified obstacles standing in the way of a Level IV connection.

Each of the six Cs is assigned a separate chapter in this section of the book. To set the stage, here is a brief description for each "C" that the StoryBranding process prescribes.

Step 1: Collect the Backstory

We start by digging up the backstory. In traditional marketing parlance, this is often referred to as the situation analysis. This provides the background necessary to explain the problem that marketing must solve. Every backstory is different but usually consists of any and all information relevant to the story about to be written. It identifies problems and opportunities that must be taken into consideration before the story unfolds.

Step 2: Characterize the Brand

This approach characterizes the brand as the hero of its own story. It is what comes to the consumer's rescue, satisfying some existing unmet need like no other. One of the key challenges of this planning process is to determine how this hero should be portrayed.

As a first step in brand planning, marketers will sometimes focus on the prospect's need and the extent to which that need is or isn't being satisfied. A process that starts by defining prospect needs may be a good way to start a new venture or to assess the potential of an invention. But for existing brands, this process differs in many ways. The Story-Branding process starts by putting the brand, not the prospect, under a microscope. Specifically, this process starts with an investigation of the brand's strengths and weaknesses in coordination with the owners and/or managers of the brand.

Once the strengths/weaknesses report card is completed, we work with the same owners and management by using a number of techniques that we will soon discuss. These are developed for the purpose of excavating values and beliefs that might otherwise be hard to articulate. We also gather wish lists for what the brand could stand for in the future. From there, we set out to match management's assessment and desires for the brand with consumer expectations. There are a number of inexpensive ways to conduct consumer research for this purpose. Having this knowledge helps us to assess just how realistic management's expectations are before a great deal of time and money is spent.

Step 3: Characterize the Prospect

Once the brand is fully characterized, then, and only then, do we look to characterize our most likely prospects. In essence, this step helps us better understand who would need what we are selling and why.

First we need to understand the functional problem that prospects are trying to solve. What must the product be able to *do* in order to satisfy or better satisfy the prospect? Out of this analysis, we can identify our most likely prospects in terms of their functional needs. But in order to make the most of our sales opportunity with this group, we need to go beyond functional needs, especially as a brand becomes more established. Specifically, we need to understand the particular beliefs and values that are drivers behind the prospect's functional needs.

For instance, we may find that a prospect needs to replace the tires on his or her car. In particular, we know our prospect is looking for a tire that will maintain traction on wet roads. Our tire may very well satisfy that functional need, but most likely other alternative brands can do the same. That being the case, we have to look beyond functional needs and identify the belief or value system underlying this need. We may find that the real motivation has something to do with the importance of safety, and this motivation is particularly important among families with children. Furthermore, we may find the importance of safety is directly related to the prospect's belief that good parents always make safety a priority above all other considerations.

For new products with unique, desirable, and discernible differences, it may be enough to sell on the basis of function alone. But sooner or later, competitive substitutes will be made available to the consumer. Before this happens, we must understand the most important set of beliefs or values that help to explain why the functional need exists. As you'll see, this will set up problems and opportunities that should be assessed when setting out to associate important meanings to a brand and in an effort to help it stand out against the backdrop of competitive substitutes.

Step 4: Connect the Characters

At this stage, we start to play matchmaker. Now that we have a deep understanding of our two characters—the brand and the prospect—we look for the fit between them. Short term, we are interested in knowing how the brand satisfies a functional need through its product features and benefits. Additionally, however, we need to know that some important shared belief or value system can spark a long-term relationship. If the values and beliefs our brand stands for do not sync with our prospects' motivating beliefs and values, we may not be going after the right prospects. However, in cases where a potential relationship has not fully reached its potential, management needs to assess the obstacles standing in the brand's way.

Step 5: Confront the Obstacles

Earlier, we defined *story* as a brand dealing with some obstacle to achieve a relationship with its prospect. In this step, we prioritize those obstacles that are keeping the brand from achieving its full potential. Our aim is to achieve what you will come to understand as a "Level IV connection"—one where customers become raving fans.

Step 6: Complete the StoryBrief

At this stage, we review the preceding steps for logical consistency and summarize them in the StoryBrief. Unlike the traditional creative brief, the StoryBrief outlines the entire brand story. To help establish some empathy for these characters, we develop what we refer to as I AM statements for each. These take the form of the prospect memoir you were introduced to in chapter 2 that was written for the prospect of Last National Bank. However, in addition to writing from the standpoint of the prospect, we also write an I AM statement as if the brand were a person. I AM statements force us to develop empathy for both characters that would otherwise be, and often are, missing in traditional creative input documents.

Additionally, we identify and prioritize the obstacles that the brand must overcome to establish a relationship with the prospect. Finally, we define the brand's unique value proposition, something that simply and succinctly summarizes the value or belief that the brand should be associated with.

SIX Cs SUMMARY

Once this process is completed, we should see an obvious consistency between all of the newly defined brand story elements. Furthermore, we will have outlined and unfolded both the plot and the theme of the brand story.

Before using the six Cs as a planning tool, you should understand that StoryBranding is both an analytical and a creative process. Structure and sequential steps are provided to guide you across the terrain. Do not hesitate to move between the steps if you need to; just strive for logical consistency. Most important, however, is that much will depend on how creative you are in identifying with both the prospect and the brand. You'll have plenty of input to help you write the I AM statements, for instance, but how you write them will have a strong influence on how well they are understood by others involved in the creation of messages. I have provided a number of guidelines and examples in chapters 16 and 17. In chapter 19, I will discuss ways in which you can test yourself.

THE 6Cs

1: COLLECT THE BACK STORY

We start by digging up the back story. In traditional marketing parlance, this is often referred to as the situation analysis. This provides the background necessary to explain the problem that must be solved for the brand. Every back story is different but usually consists of any and all information relevant to the story about to be written. This includes an assessment of the brand's culture as well as problems and opportunities it faces in the marketplace.

2: CHARACTERIZE THE BRAND

Traditional planning methods start by focusing on the prospect. The StoryBranding process starts first with an investigation of the brand. Specifically, it starts with a thorough understanding of the brand's value and belief system and how this is supported. Is what the brand stands for being evidenced? Additionally, we look to make certain that there is discernable and genuine proof behind what the brand stands for. Most important, will prospects resist or subscribe to certain associations that the brand would like to take on?

3: CHARACTERIZE THE PROSPECT

Once the brand is fully explored, we then look to the prospect for insight. Specifically, we look to see what functional and emotional needs are being left unfulfilled. Then we set out to discover the extent to which any of these needs presents an opportunity for the brand in question.

4: CONNECT THE CHARACTERS

At this stage, we start to play matchmaker. Now that we understand our two story characters, the brand and the prospect, we look for the fit between them. Short term, we are interested in knowing how the brand satisfies a functional need through its product features and benefits. Additionally, however, we need to know that there is something that can spark a long-term relationship, one that is founded on shared values and beliefs.

5: CONFRONT THE OBSTACLES

Our model requires a definition of the communication obstacles standing in the way of the brand/prospect relationship. Typically these fall into four categories: awareness, comprehension, association, and affinity. The extent to which any of these obstacles must be overcome sets up the plot. Besides identifying the big rocks that are in the way, we prioritize them in order of which have to be moved first to achieve the brand's ultimate relationship goal.

6: COMPLETE THE STORY BRIEF

At this stage, we review the preceding steps for logical consistency and summarize them in the StoryBrief. Unlike the traditional creative brief, the StoryBrief outlines the entire brand story. It identifies the inner and outer layers of our two characters: the brand and the prospect. Once this process is completed, we should see a logical consistency between all of the newly defined brand story elements. Furthermore, we will have outlined and unfolded both the plot and the theme of the brand story.

Review

- The StoryBranding process is, in effect, the assembly line for component parts of the brand story.

- The six Cs of the StoryBranding process are:

    - Collect the Backstory

    - Characterize the Brand

    - Characterize the Prospect

    - Connect the Characters

    - Confront the Obstacles

    - Complete the StoryBrief

- Once this process is completed, there should be a logical consistency between all six Cs.

CHAPTER 7

Once Upon a Time . . .

Every story would be another story, and unrecognizable as art, if it took up its characters and plot and happened somewhere else.
—*Eudora Welty, American author of short stories and novels*

The brand's backstory describes when, where, and why the story takes place. It also identifies the reason for the story being written in the first place, as it defines the problems and opportunities for the main characters of our story: the brand hero and its beneficiary, the prospect. The backstory is often referred to in marketing circles as the situation analysis. In every sense, this description is apt. The backstory provides a snapshot of the brand's situation while analyzing how it got there.

We see the backstory as the brand's story, thus far. In piecing together the backstory, we ask, "What is the brand's current situation and how did it get that way?"

We divide the backstory into three sections: "In the beginning"; "Then what?"; and "And now?"

In the beginning: Inevitably we start at the start, with the history of how the brand began, who started it, and why. What was the original vision? Does this vision remain the same today? If not, why not?

Then what?: If the brand has a history, was the brand a smashing success from the start? If not, what got in the way? How did the brand change, improve, or even degenerate into what it is today?

And now?: The And now section of the backstory is perhaps the most important since this is where we get handed the baton. Based on what we know about the past, if there is one, it is our job to move the brand story forward.

Typically, a standard SWOT (Strengths, Weaknesses, Opportunities, Threats) analysis will unveil important issues. Alternatively, one might complete an analysis of the brand's four Ps (product, price, place, and promotion). It is assumed that anyone reading this book is familiar with a situation analysis and the various ways it can be approached from a marketing perspective. I've opted not to rehash detailed situation analysis checklists that are often provided in marketing textbooks. These can also be found by searching the Internet. Another suggestion is to account for the Five Forces devised by Michael E. Porter from the Harvard Business School.

Instead, and given the goal of StoryBranding to create a strong and enduring relationship with the prospect, I want to focus attention on the brand and the prospect the way an author might attend to the makeup of his or her characters.

First, while describing the backstory, and especially for service companies, we put a great deal of stock in our observations. Specifically we are interested in the culture of the company that produces the brand. In turn, we act the part of corporate anthropologists to assess the company's values, customs, and traditions. Certainly, much of the information we are interested in will come from interviews with management, but more of it comes from what we see than from what we hear.

For instance, we like to consider what the offices look like. How are people dressed? How do we characterize the people as they interact with each other? Does the company rely on formal or informal channels of communication? Is the company's tone serious or is it more laid-back? What kinds of pictures or company information is found on the walls?

Additionally, what are the company's rites and rituals? How are employees recognized, if they are? Do they subscribe to any mottos or sayings? What is management's assessment of its employees, and what are the employees' assessments of management? Answers to questions like these can help determine important beliefs and values that affect the way the brand is produced and marketed.

In addition to looking over the company's employee handbook, we will sometimes conduct one-on-one interviews with randomly selected employees from all departments. In these interviews we ask them to bring in pictures from magazines and/or Google searches that describe the company. In asking them to explain why particular pictures were selected, we are able to extract a great deal of hidden information about what is important to the company and its people.

We are interested in how people advance through the company and how often employees leave. What kinds of people does the company hire and who are considered *fast trackers*? Where are the power pockets within the company? Where do marketing personnel fall within the pecking order relative to operations and financial people? What is the CEO's background? What is the CMO's background?

We'll sometimes ask people to use metaphors to describe their company; for example, what kind of animal, car, or celebrity does the company act like? We will also try to determine who the role models are, or who the employees see as company heroes. Language is also a signpost of the company's culture. Is there an overreliance on acronyms, metaphors, or jargon? Is the language informal or formal? What is taboo within the company? What is laudable?

In addition to observation, survey assessments can be helpful as well. A large number of standard employee assessments are available to help define a company's culture. One in particular, developed by Denison Consulting called DOCS (for Denison Organizational Cultural Survey), measures the link between organizational culture and bottom-line performance such as return on investment, sales growth, quality, innovation, and employee satisfaction. For more information, go to www.Denison-consulting.com.

Again, this chapter by no means is intended to provide a comprehensive list of questions that should be asked to construct the backstory for either the brand or prospect. Many traditional marketing texts and Internet resources have checklists if you need them. My purpose here is merely to say that some sort of audit should be conducted to ascertain information about history, the recent past, and the present. More often than not, the challenge isn't gathering information as much as it is sifting through it for relevancy.

Review

- The purpose of the backstory is to describe the brand's unique situation from its origins to where it is now.

- The *And now* section of the backstory is perhaps the most important, since this is where we get handed the baton. Based on what we know about the past, it is our job to move the brand story forward.

- To develop the backstory, we act the part of corporate anthropologists to assess the company's values, customs, and traditions.

CHAPTER 8

Brand First

Success means never letting the competition define you. Instead you have to define yourself based on a point of view you care deeply about.
—Tom Chappell, Tom's of Maine

One day while I was attending a college introductory marketing class, the professor asked me to define "marketing concept" in front of the class. Not having been fully prepared (well, not having been at all prepared), I stood up and sheepishly answered, "Buy low, sell high?"

The next person the professor called on bounced out of his chair with a hey-anyone-should-be-able-to-answer-that-one swagger. And after the professor showered him with high praise, my embarrassment morphed into humiliation. I have never forgotten the marketing concept. More than thirty years later, I can still recite it verbatim: *Firms should analyze the needs of their customers first before making decisions about how to satisfy those needs better than their competitors.* Shame is an underrated memorization aid.

The marketing concept suggests a two-step sequential ordering of how marketing is done. "Analyze the needs of customers and do this *before* making decisions on how to satisfy those needs." This was religion. The companies that followed this sequence were destined for marketing heaven. *Production-oriented* marketers, or those who reversed the order, would be banished to marketing hell. Some thirty years later, however, I've become the Martin Luther of the marketing concept.

For new brands or those without an established identity, surveying consumer needs before betting the farm on a new invention makes a great deal of sense. However, for the majority of brands that fall somewhere between the relatively new and the barely staying alive, I'd strongly recommend avoiding the marketing concept.

The marketing concept comes from a one-sided notion that "the customer is king." So find out what the king needs first, then satisfy the king. The marketing concept suggests that to think marketing should be done any other way is blasphemous. But sin with me just for a moment. Confession is optional.

First, consider New Coke. In taste tests conducted throughout the world, the king said, "Wow, this tastes better than the old stuff. Bring it on!" But when Coke introduced it, the king got very upset. "How could Coke abandon its very rich heritage?" the king said.

Oldsmobile had a long-standing position as the upper-middle-class Cadillac. The king said, "Your car is for old people. You need to make it more youthful." So Olds reintroduced itself as "Not Your Father's Oldsmobile." Clever line. But RIP Oldsmobile.

Gap tried to change its logo to reflect more of what the king said he wanted: a transition from classic to cool and sexy. After being ridiculed by the king over the Internet for changing the logo, Gap's spokesperson lamented, "[We] learned just how much energy there is around our brand, and after much thought, we've decided to go back to our iconic blue box logo."*

KFC discovered that the king was becoming more health conscious and was telling KFC to get with it. "You guys are selling fried chicken. That's not healthy." So KFC ran ads that said, "Hey, King, Unthink KFC. We are now emphasizing our new grilled chicken." "Great," the king said, but then stopped going to KFC as often.

Whenever I give these examples of marketing mistakes, I get one or two "yeah buts." "Yeah but" they defined the king wrong, or "yeah but" they didn't ask the king the right questions. And to this, I rejoin with my own "yeah but": It doesn't matter. In all cases, the brand forgot something very important. Regardless of what the king says he wants, there's only so much change a brand can make, given who the brand is. Marketing conceptors say, study the king first. StoryBranders say, study your brand first.

FIRST THINGS LAST

Writers, at least the best among them, do not start by conducting focus groups to help them decide between genres or story themes. Doris Kearns Goodwin isn't going to stop writing historical fiction and Philip Roth isn't going to start writing Harlequin novels because a reader survey says doing so would help them sell more books. Certainly, we ultimately need to understand the who, the where, and the what about prospects that will attract them to the brand. But considerations can get

---

* "Gap abandons widely despised logo update," Oct. 12, 2010, www.mediabistro.com.

in the way, up front. Stephen King was once asked to comment on a story he had read.

"No," he moaned. "It's not a very good story. Its author was too busy listening to other voices as closely as he should have to the one coming from inside."

BRAND FIRST

The StoryBranding process does what is prescribed by the marketing concept in reverse. Instead of beginning the planning process by focusing on customer needs, we start by looking at the brand first, from the inside out, in order to discover what the brand stands for.

Established brands, by definition, have meanings that are well entrenched both inside and outside their organizations. We start by understanding brand meaning internally. And we start by excavating the brand's meaning from its own expert cultural historians: management and employees. We often do this with the help of some tools you'll soon be introduced to later in this section, tools that facilitate an articulation of the brand's meaning, which is sometimes hard to achieve with words alone.

This is not to suggest that consumer research should be discouraged at this point in the process. However, if conducted, any research should help management determine how close or far away their intended associations with the brand are to consumer associations. Research should provide a feedback function and stop there.

"WHAT IF WE NEED TO CHANGE?"

As you've seen from previous examples, consumer value associations become barnacled to brand identities over time. And once they grab hold, they rarely let go. So what does a brand do when it determines that sales declines can be attributed to an old identity that is no longer relevant?

Imagine, if you will, a 10-point scale, where 1 is labeled "Incremental Change" and 10 is labeled "Fundamental Change." Depending on how well entrenched your brand's identity, acceptable and believable change will fall somewhere between these two extremes.

For mature brands especially, it is very difficult, if not impossible, to affect a fundamental change in a brand's identity. Try as you might, it's hard to "unring a bell." Furthermore, the extent to which the existing identity is entrenched will have a major impact on how much incremental change is possible.

Before racing headlong into changing your brand's identity, assess the risks associated with the proposed change, both in terms of upside potential and downside loss. Chicken Little forecasts by management that "we must change our identity or we're going to perish," should be thought through carefully. More often than not, the only thing that needs to change is an improved sense of the beliefs and values that haven't changed. The challenge is to help management find the internalized value that continues to power the brand's engine. And this challenge must be undertaken first before any attempts are made to connect with the prospect. Oftentimes it comes down to good judgment. However, if in doubt, any number of research companies can help with this assessment.

In any case, however, some change can always be made, however slight. Ideally, you'll want to make as little change as possible in order to effect as big a turnaround as possible. There's no need to go for fundamental change when an incremental change will do.

What you may find out is that the brand merely needs to emphasize different aspects of its existing identity or to recast who it is in a way that is more relevant for the times. A recent campaign by Old Spice demonstrates just how this is done. Old Spice is the Oldsmobile campaign done right.

I distinctly remember listening to my dad shave every morning as I lay in bed waiting to use the bathroom. It got so that I could predict the exact time when I'd hear the *slap, slap, slap* of his hands to his cheeks as he would apply Old Spice aftershave. If I walked in on him, he'd put some on me, and all day I'd think I was like him. For me, Old Spice was part of a masculine ritual that would someday be mine. Old Spice capitalized on the value of manhood. But unlike Oldsmobile, which tried to modernize its outer layer, Old Spice merely contemporized its inner value. It didn't apologize for what it has always stood for. Instead Old Spice introduced the mantra, "Smell Like a Man," thereby associating itself with the core value of masculinity but in the context of the twenty-first century.

Another example is Abercrombie & Fitch. Its flagship store on New York's Fifth Avenue binds the company's legacy as a purveyor of outdoor paraphernalia with its role as a modern-day hangout for teens buying jeans and T-shirts. There you'll see a moosehead mounted over the cashier's counter, wooden canoes with dark lighting, and after-hours dance club music playing throughout the store.

Generally speaking, it is always better for a brand to find a way to change within the context of inherent values rather than to adopt a whole new set. In this way, the brand can become more relevant for the times while remaining true to its well-known heritage.

X MARKS THE SPOT

Characterizing a brand is similar to looking for the X that marks "YOU ARE HERE" on one of those store directories at the shopping mall. Nobody knows where the brand's X is any better than management. If there's disagreement as to where that X is, management must first work toward better internal alignment.

However, if you're thinking your brand's functional features and benefits mark the X, you need to keep looking. What you've found is the brand's outer layer. And if you stop your search here, you could run into dangers down the road. Once a brand becomes defined solely by its outer layer, it's hard for consumers to see that brand any other way.

Consider Xerox. Xerox associated itself with copiers. That's what it was. When Xerox tried to introduce a computer, we resisted. Their identity as a copier manufacturer would not allow us to see them any other way. Burger King introduced itself as the place where you can have a burger prepared your way. At the time this idea provided them with a great functional difference from other fast food restaurants. On the other hand McDonald's, since its early beginnings, has consistently associated itself with the values of food, folks, and fun. Is it any wonder Burger King has never been able to catch up to McDonald's? Once its functional selling proposition became passé, Burger King lost its edge.

Similarly, Domino's claim to fame was that it could deliver pizzas in thirty minutes, guaranteed. Ever since thirty-minute pizza deliveries have become a parity, Domino's has struggled with its identity.

These are examples of the Level I and II ruts I spoke of earlier.

Contrast these examples with Nike, a brand that has achieved a Level IV connection with many of its customers. Nike is much more than a maker of running shoes. From its early beginnings, Nike set out to associate itself with the belief that athletic performance is a function of persistence and dedication. This idea was easily extended to all forms of athletic gear and sportswear that carry the Nike brand. The same with Apple. Apple isn't just a computer. Over time it has become associated with independence and creativity. This association manifests itself in any number of information products it continues to regularly introduce.

Another example is Google. Google isn't just a search engine; it's an information force that continues to grow with products that are well aligned with this association.

That said, don't walk away from the importance of your brand's outer layer. It can provide valuable clues on where to find that X. By working backward from the functions your product performs, you may be able to better understand your brand's underlying motivation for existing.

In a recent assignment, we worked with a brand that had become well established as the discount alternative within its category. As costs were increasing, the brand needed to increase its margins in order to grow. Together with management, we worked backward from their "discounter" outer layer function toward finding the underlying human value that was the source of their discounting. We determined that this brand could best be identified and supported by management as one that placed fairness and integrity above all else. With advertising that supported this brand's inner-layer association with fairness, rather than its price-per-item outer-layer discount claim, we were able to appeal to consumers who shared that value for fairness. In turn, a more emotional appeal allowed the brand to raise prices incrementally while continuing to meet consumer expectations that their prices would always be lower than the competition.

ART OR SCIENCE?

Many planning processes start out as science before the artists get a say. StoryBranding starts out as art before the scientists have their say. Traditional approaches that first take a look at what consumers want and need can lead a brand astray. The StoryBranding approach is based on the premise that brands should strive for authenticity. And authenticity is found in consistent adherence to strongly held values and beliefs, not in values and beliefs that are manufactured or changed simply because of a newly foreseen opportunity.

Sometimes pegged as radical, in reality StoryBranding springs from a more conservative foundation. It is based on the premise that overhauling a brand's identity should not be taken lightly. Rather than throwing out the old identity, one should embrace it, accept it, and figure out how to evolve it.

Review

- For new products, surveying consumer needs before betting on them makes a great deal of sense. However, for the brands that fall somewhere between the new and the barely staying alive, it's important to break away from the stranglehold that assessing customer needs first (as prescribed by "the marketing concept") can potentially put on a brand.

- Storywriters, at least the best among them, do not start by conducting focus groups to help them decide between genres or story themes.

- Certainly, we ultimately need to understand who and where the most likely prospects are for the purposes of shaping and marketing the brand's stories. But those considerations can get in the way up front.

- The StoryBranding process does what is prescribed by the marketing concept but in reverse. Instead of beginning the planning process by focusing on customer needs, we start by concentrating on what the brand currently stands for.

- Especially for mature products, the traditional marketing concept can lead marketers toward positioning their brands as something they are not.

- StoryBranding is based on a premise that brands should strive for authenticity. The main ingredient of authenticity is knowing who the brand is in addition to what the brand does.

- To maintain its integrity, a brand must remain true to itself from the start.

CHAPTER 9

The Brand's Inner Layer

*Once you think of a brand as a belief system, you automatically get all
the things that enterprise spends billions of dollars trying to obtain:
trust, relevance, vision, values, leadership.*
—Patrick Hanlon, *Primal Branding*

Another way to think of your brand's inner layer is to think of it as your
brand's soul. By contrast, the outer layer is its body and behaves according to beliefs and values that are directed by the brand's inner layer.

As discussed in the previous chapter, StoryBranding advocates a
"brand first" approach for the purpose of arriving at an authentic story,
meaning that management, *not* the voice of the consumer, should determine what the inner layer is comprised of and that it should reflect
genuine, rather than synthetic, values.

The purpose of this chapter is to expand on the concept of the
brand's inner layer, to better familiarize you with both its function and
purpose.

When we first introduced you to the six Cs of the StoryBranding Process, we showed how the brand is cast as hero of its own story.

Some, in fact many, marketers will vehemently argue that the hero should always be the customer. Hopefully by now you've seen examples of what happens when the brand relinquishes hero status to the customer. It's one thing to believe that customer satisfaction is something worth striving toward at all times. But when a brand puts its customers and prospects in the driver's seat to determine what the brand stands for, the results can be disastrous.

What we are looking for within the brand's inner layer is not a product or service advantage or benefit. We are looking for belief in something very important, and one that explains the why behind those features and benefits. In effect, we are looking for the brand's cause. I am sometimes asked if the inner layer is nothing more than the brand's mission statement. Please note: A mission statement is *not* what I'm referring to. If you can remember one thing from this chapter on the brand's inner layer, remember this: A mission statement provides the rational purpose of the brand. The brand's unique value is what drives that purpose.

I am not discounting the importance of a mission statement. Clearly, every company/brand should have one. But mission statements are notoriously vague, often provide little emotional traction, and are unoriginal. Case in point is this one from a very large brand: "[We] continuously strive to meet the needs of customers for total value by offering a unique package of location, price, service, and assortment." I just hope their *unique package* is more unique than their mission statement.

Books, websites, and many consulting services will provide advice on how to write a mission statement. Many have differing opinions of what a mission statement is or should be. My purpose is not to get into that fray but instead to say that mission statements are not necessarily the unique value propositions (UVPs) briefly discussed in chapter 3. As you will see when we start applying certain principles used to write UVPs, they are sometimes stated as a belief, e.g., "We believe in supporting the few who courageously display their individuality," or "The purpose of

invention is important, but purposeful invention is critical." Sometimes
the UVP is expressed as a mantra or a call to action: "Never avoid doing
things the hard way when the hard way is the best way." Sometimes the
UVP sounds and looks like an advertising theme line, for example, "Be
All That You Can Be" or "Think Different." In fact, UVPs sometimes
make great theme lines. Just keep in mind that they are never claims.
Claims present arguments. Stories don't argue or debate to win their
audiences' favor. Rather, they invite compliance and leave conclusions
to interpretation.

I'll be discussing both UVP statements and advertising theme lines
in later chapters with examples of each. But for now, just know that a
UVP sharply and authentically states the unique belief that a brand can
and should be associated with. Moreover, any UVP must be real from
the inside out.

ANATOMY OF A BRAND HERO

The hero of any story is the person who resolves the tension created by
the story's conflict. In fairy tales, the hero might be the dragon slayer or
the white knight who comes to the rescue of the damsel in distress. In
literature and movies, the hero might be the person who takes action
against some evil. The hero can be the main character of the story solving his or her own problem or someone who solves the problem for
someone else. But either way, the hero, by resolving the story's conflict,
facilitates the lesson or message of the story.

Whether it's Aesop's slow but steady tortoise or Hemingway's per-
sistent old fisherman of the sea, lessons are passed on to us through
heroes. They embody values and beliefs that the author deems important
enough to write about.

All heroes have attributes and capabilities that allow them to accomplish both mental and physical feats. But whether the hero can leap tall

buildings in a single bound, outwit a captor, or conquer a lifelong fear, what and how the hero resolves the story's problem is not nearly as emotionally engaging as why solving the problem is important in the first place. We can perhaps aspire to the physical and mental accomplishments of heroes, but the reason we cheer them on has little to do with their abilities relative to what we believe are their motivations. We relate to heroes because we can somehow identify with the driving force behind what they are trying to accomplish. Whether it's fighting crime, beating a drug habit, or ending loneliness, our connection with the hero is not in what is being done as much as why it is being done.

Often, our connection to the hero is not something we are fully aware of. It often grabs us unconsciously. But the intensity of our connection is in direct proportion to how important a similar motivation works in our own lives. As interesting as the ability to fly through forests might be, I can't relate to Jake Sully's ability to do so in James Cameron's *Avatar*. But I can relate to Sully's need to rise above misunderstandings and his desire to bring peace to the lives of his people. Value identification, not ability identification, is at the base of any emotional connection we have with a story hero.

WHERE DO MOTIVATIONS COME FROM?

Man is what he believes. —*Anton Chekhov*

Underneath every motivation is a value or belief in some idea that is important. Love, fun, accomplishment, belonging, justice, recognition, etc., propel us to behave the way we do. They also help us form relationships. Shared values are the foundations of governments, religions, cultures, marriages, friendships, and, oh yeah, brands. Both the intensity and number of shared values explain the importance of any relationship we have with other individuals, groups, or possessions. If our shared values are inconsequential, so is our relationship. On the other hand, shared values that are considered important serve as the basis for strong friendships, marriages, and group affiliations.

FROM STORY HERO TO BRAND HERO

It is similar with brands and how we regard or relate to them. The extent and the intensity of our emotional connection to a brand is a function of how important the value is that the brand symbolizes. This explains why some people will pay for what could amount to a lifetime supply of Bic pens to own a Mont Blanc pen, even though both perform the same function. This explains why supermarket shoppers will pay more for branded salt than a generic equivalent even though salt is salt.

When MP3 players were introduced, I purchased one made by RIO, a relatively unknown brand. I didn't care about the brand's meaning as much as I cared about the brand's function or its ability to make my music collection portable (a Level I connection). But as more MP3 players came on the market, the idea of owning one made by Apple appealed to me, and I eventually switched from my RIO. I switched despite the fact that both the RIO and the iPod were functionally similar. For me, the values that Apple represented far outweighed any functional considerations given to any other brand of players. In fact, I paid more to own an Apple iPod than I would have paid for a similar product made by RIO, Microsoft, Creative Labs, or any other manufacturer of MP3 players. The iPod allowed me to wear those white headphones that communicated my story to anyone who saw me. My Level IV connection with Apple is what continues to motivate me to prefer any product made by Apple.

Especially among business-to-business marketers, sometimes little or no consideration is given to a brand's value association. They stall out at the Level II or III connection milestones. As I witnessed while working at an agency that specialized in business-to-business advertising, it was rare to work with clients interested in digging any deeper for the brand's meaning beyond left-brain, rational benefits like reduced downtime, quality parts, or increased ROI. B2B marketers often see their buyers as highly rational and thus spend an inordinate amount of time and money trying to outshout their competitor's benefit claims with charts, graphs, numbers, and awards.

This is not to diminish the importance for brands to prove product performance when purchase risks are high, as is often the case in B2B situations. But until computers make all the buying decisions, human beings will always buy for emotional reasons and justify their purchases for rational reasons. In the end, values such as trust, confidence, status, security, and innovation are much stronger purchase motivators, regardless of any facts that support product superiority.

Another reason why value differences are more important than functional differences is that functional differences have expiration dates. We live in a version 2.0 world. Today's features that allow the brand to boast about unique selling propositions (e.g., faster, cheaper, or longer lasting) are tomorrow's also-rans. On the other hand, defining a brand's UVP is defining a matchless value or a universal truth that the brand upholds. Once a brand puts a stake in the ground demonstrating what its ultimate truth is while resonating with consumers who also sub-scribe to or identify with that truth, competitors cannot copy it with-out appearing imitative. Furthermore, once the brand's unique value proposition is established, it no longer has to depend solely on here-today-gone-tomorrow performance superiority claims. A trusted brand or one that the consumer can connect with emotionally is given strong purchase consideration, regardless of competitive claims. The stronger the connection, the stronger the guard against competitive inroads.

THE CHALLENGE TO FIND MEANING

Whether we're talking about B2B or B2C brands, both are faced with the same meaning challenge. Management teams in both environments work day in and day out with numbers and the tools of logic and analytics. Understandably, they have a hard time tapping into the inner layer where the more emotional, nonlinear, softer stuff of a brand's meaning resides.

Brands, like heroes, are complex and are driven by numerous values. Finding the single value that is most *true* within an organization—the one that both consumers and employees will emotionally connect with— is one of the most difficult challenges facing any brand manufacturer or provider. Management, given its rational proclivities, needs the right tools to mirror the single most important value that distinguishes their brand against the backdrop of competitors. Distinguishing this value can be accomplished in a number of ways. But we have found a way that has proven to work time and time again. It's called archetypal analysis.

Review

- The brand's inner layer is really the mind or soul of the brand. It houses the brand's intention, which is composed of beliefs and values that it champions.

- The inner layer is determined by management through an analysis of history, resources, trends, and vision, not through directions dictated by customer surveys.

- The crown of authenticity is bestowed upon the self-directed brands, those that are true to themselves, those whose actions say more than their words.

- Without knowing the beliefs that management wants associated with its brand, the brand's reason for being is nothing more than a profit motive, and that will never be enough if management expects the brand to survive.

- A unique value proposition (UVP) sharply and authentically states the unique belief that a brand should be/can be associated with. It must be real from the inside out.

- We can perhaps aspire to the physical and mental accomplishments of heroes, but the reason we cheer them on has little to do with their abilities relative to what we believe are their motivations.

- The extent and the intensity of our emotional connection to a brand is a function of how important the value is that the brand symbolizes.

- Until computers make all the buying decisions, human beings will always buy for emotional reasons and justify their purchases for rational reasons.

- One reason value differences are more important than functional differences is that functional differences have expiration dates.

- Management, given their rational proclivities, need the right tools to mirror the single most important value that distinguishes their brand against the backdrop of competitors.

CHAPTER 10

Using Archetypal Analysis

A brand is a metaphorical story that connects with something very deep—
a fundamental human appreciation of mythology ... Companies that
manifest this sensibility invoke something very powerful.
—Scott Bedbury, *former head of marketing for Nike and Starbucks*

It is one thing to know what the brand's inner layer consists of. It is quite another to articulate it. Following the procedure outlined in chapter 6, and before moving on to identify communication obstacles, it is important to arrive at a workable definition for the inner layer. Language is a funny thing. Words expressed provide concrete frames of reference that help us to define problems and see solutions hiding from our own awareness. In other words, we sometimes have to hear ourselves say what we mean before we can know what we mean. The act of articulating our thoughts often changes our thoughts. To help define the brand's inner layer, we use what is referred to as archetypal analysis. The goal of archetypal analysis is to give us the language, the frames of reference we need to bring the brand's meaning out of hiding.

Carl Jung, the legendary psychologist, first applied the term "archetypes" to describe universal behavioral patterns in all stories regardless of their cultural or historical period. He identified these repeating behaviors with story character descriptions and suggested that they are all found to greater or lesser degrees in all human behavior. Understanding what these archetypes are and how they influence our behavior helps us understand the values that motivate us to behave the way we do. Likewise, thinking of the brand as a person, we use archetypes to analyze a brand's inner layer, or the driving force behind why it does what it does, beyond the profit motive.

Archetypal analysis can be somewhat mystical and mysterious. The first time I raised the issue of archetypes with a client, he rolled his eyes and asked if we were going to be burning incense and conjuring spirits. But in our research on stories, I found that archetypal analysis is one of the most common forms of literary analysis. Don't worry, we're not going to go too deep into the weeds here. The subject of archetypes is vast and far beyond what we can cover in just one chapter. But we will cover enough to be practical and useful.

Wikipedia describes an archetype as "an original model of a person, ideal example, or a prototype after which others are copied, patterned, or emulated; a symbol universally recognized by all." In other words, an archetype refers to a generic version of a personality. In this sense, *mother figure* may be considered an archetype and may be identified in various characters with distinct personalities.

Archetypes are also found in us to various degrees. Each of us operates on the basis of one or more dominant archetypes. If you're interested in finding out what yours are, I recommend that you take the PMAI (Pearson–Marr Archetypal Indicator that you can self-administer by logging into www.capt.org/. I took the test and found it to be very helpful in understanding myself and the way I communicate with others, but that's another story [and what a story it is]).

Using archetypes is a radical departure from traditional ways of understanding brands. But then again, StoryBranding is a radical departure from traditional brand-planning approaches.

COMMON CHARACTER ARCHETYPES

Opinions differ on how many archetypes should be used for marketing purposes. One source lists more than fifty. Another, more than a hundred. Carol S. Pearson and Margaret Mark list a dozen in their book *The Hero and the Outlaw*, which is considered by many to be the seminal work on brand archetypes. Drawing from a number of sources, we have identified twelve distinct archetypes that are variations of those posited by Pearson and Mark. Each, as you will see, champions a different human value. On the following pages, each is identified in ways that can be applied to brands. To enhance readability, I've given them all a masculine gender, as in *he*, *him*, or *his*, but all archetypes are gender neutral.

THE PURIST

Simply and virtuously, the Purist is wholesome, exemplary, and highly ethical. He believes in being good and doing good.

SAYINGS A PURIST MIGHT LIVE BY:

- "Look at everything through kindly eyes."
- "Nice guys finish first."
- "Do the right thing, even when no one is looking."

CHAMPIONS VALUES SUCH AS:

Harmony, Peace, Optimism, Simplicity, Purity, Innocence, Honesty, Happiness, Faith

DISDAINS:

- Deception
- Discord
- Complication
- War
- Behaving in an Unacceptable Manner

OPPOSITES:

- Negativity
- Prejudice
- Evil

PEOPLE:

Julie Andrews, Mr. Rogers, Michael J. Fox, Princess Diana, Audrey Hepburn

FOR BRANDS THAT:

are associated with simplicity, purity, health, and good simple living

BRANDS:

Disney, Dove, H2O, Make-A-Wish Foundation, Sesame Street, Brita Water Purifiers, Whole Foods

THE PIONEER

The Pioneer is an individualist, blazing his own trail in pursuit of freedom, adventure, and new experiences that feed his soul. Whether gearing up to climb Mount Everest or going off in a Jeep Wrangler, the Pioneer looks for brands that allow him to experience life to the fullest. The Pioneer is usually an early adopter of invention.

SAYINGS A PIONEER MIGHT LIVE BY:

- "I'll sleep when I'm dead."
- "The journey is more important than the destination."
- "Because it's there."

CHAMPIONS VALUES SUCH AS:

Exploration, Freedom, Adventure, Independence, Experimentation, Self reliance, Ambition, Challenge, Bravery, Confidence

DISDAINS:

- Boundaries
- Boredom
- Limitations
- Stagnation

OPPOSITES:

- Complacency
- Conformity
- Avoidance

PEOPLE: Amelia Earhart, Christopher Columbus, Neil Armstrong, Billy Jean King, Stephen Hawking

FOR BRANDS THAT:

foster discovery

BRANDS:

Groupon, Trader Joe's, The North Face, Jeep, Discovery Channel

THE ENTERTAINER

The Entertainer is your typical clown or prankster—a fun-loving free spirit who wants only to live in the moment and have a good time doing it. He has a unique ability to capture and transfix an audience's attention. He enjoys brands that employ humor and promise fun times.

SAYINGS AN ENTERTAINER MIGHT LIVE BY:

- "Laughter is the best medicine."
- "The most wasted of all days is one without laughter."
- "A man isn't poor if he can still laugh."

CHAMPIONS VALUES SUCH AS:

Humor, Spontaneity, Charm, Youthfulness, Laughter, Gregariousness, Levity, Happiness, Fun

DISDAINS:

- Seriousness
- Gravity
- Tragedy
- Depression
- Boredom

OPPOSITES:

- Humorlessness
- Stoicism
- Puritanism
- Sadness

PEOPLE: Jerry Lewis, Robin Williams, Steve Martin, Jerry Seinfeld, Jim Carrey

FOR BRANDS THAT:

help customers enjoy themselves through fun and humor

BRANDS:

Bazooka Bubble Gum, Dr. Pepper, Jack in the Box, Looney Tunes, Doritos, M&M's, Comedy Central, Snickers, Bud Light

THE CONQUEROR

The Conqueror is noble and is identified by an ability to meet and overcome adversity. He is steadfast when meeting challenges head on, no matter how difficult. He is relentless, resilient, and confident in his abilities, and feels that anything he earns is well deserved.

SAYINGS A CONQUERER MIGHT LIVE BY:

- "Winning is everything."
- "Winning takes talent; to repeat takes character."

CHAMPIONS VALUES SUCH AS:

Courage, Determination, Endurance, Persistence, Success, Elitism, Strength, Status, Honor

DISDAINS:

- Weakness
- Self Doubt
- Defeat
- Vulnerability

OPPOSITES:

- Fearfulness
- Selfishness
- Cowardice
- Pessimism
- Giving Up
- Failure

PEOPLE: Vince Lombardi, Lance Armstrong, Michael Jordan

FOR BRANDS THAT:

challenge, inspire, and empower peak performance

BRANDS:

The Marines, Nike, Weight Watchers, Gatorade

THE WIZARD

The Wizard seeks out experiences that transform the ordinary into the extraordinary. He represents the universal message of mystery, thrill, and novelty. The Wizard seeks experiences that make his dreams come true, whether it's the wonder of technology that never quits, magical potions that fight the effects of aging, or a golden passport to all the world has to offer.

SAYINGS A WIZARD MIGHT LIVE BY:

- "Anything is possible."
- "Dreams do come true."
- "Wonders never cease."

CHAMPIONS VALUES SUCH AS:

Magic, Imagination, Joy, Curiosity, Optimism, Fun, Surprise

DISDAINS:

- Ordinariness
- Failure
- Status Quo
- Ineffectiveness

OPPOSITES:

- Boredom
- Same ole same ole
- Pessimism
- Lifelessness
- Negativity

PEOPLE: Steven Spielberg, George Lucas, Harry Potter, Billy Mays, The Wizard of Oz, Steve Jobs

FOR BRANDS THAT:

transform and create miracles

BRANDS:

Pixar, Lotto, Viagra, Cirque Du Soleil, Disney World, Apple

THE PROTECTOR

The Protector values compassion and generosity. He puts others first, providing tender loving care, support, and reassurance.

SAYINGS A PROTECTOR MIGHT LIVE BY:

- "Love thy neighbor."
- "Take care of yourself."
- "Lead by compassion."

CHAMPIONS VALUES SUCH AS:

Compassion, Motherly Advice, Hospitality, Protection, Comfort, Empathy, Generosity, Thoughtfulness, Sincerity, Sharing, Warmth, Wisdom

DISDAINS:

- Cruelty
- Hatred
- Bitterness
- Harshness

OPPOSITES:

- Carelessness
- Selfishness

PEOPLE: Florence Henderson, Mother Teresa, Andy Griffith, Florence Nightingale

FOR BRANDS THAT:

are caring and nurturing, providing comfort and peace of mind when customers especially need it

BRANDS:

Gerber, Cracker Barrel, Campbell's Soup, Allstate, Johnson & Johnson, Kraft

THE SEDUCER

The Seducer unsurprisingly desires romance, intimacy, and sensual pleasure. He's not afraid to indulge and especially enjoys products and brands that hold strong sex appeal and that promise to boost attractiveness and desirability.

SAYINGS A SEDUCER MIGHT LIVE BY:

- "Love conquers all."
- "All you need is love."
- "A little romance goes a long way."

CHAMPIONS VALUES SUCH AS:

Love, Sensuality, Affection, Intimacy, Beauty, Passion, Desire, Ecstasy, Connection, Enjoyment, Pleasure

DISDAINS:

- Solitude
- Unattractiveness
- Plainness

OPPOSITES:

- Hate
- Brute Force
- Purity

PEOPLE: Marilyn Monroe, Hugh Hefner, Bo Derek, Scarlett Johansson

FOR BRANDS THAT:

provide a sense of romance, connection, and sensual enjoyment

BRANDS:

Victoria's Secret, Godiva, De Beers, Courvoisier, Axe, 1-800-FLOWERS.COM

THE IMAGINEER

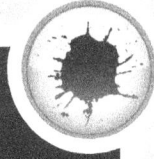

The Imagineer is an artist, an innovator, and a dreamer. He summons artistry and imagination to express himself and his vision of the world.

SAYINGS AN IMAGINEER MIGHT LIVE BY:

- "Imagination is possibility."
- "What you believe can be conceived."
- "Life is but a dream."

CHAMPIONS VALUES SUCH AS:

Creativity, Passion, Ingenuity, Vision, Creation, Innovation, Originality, Uniqueness, Artistry, Independent thinking

DISADAINS:

- Constraint
- Order
- Structure
- Boredom
- Sameness
- The Expected
- Limitations
- Directives

OPPOSITES:

- Traditionalist
- Fundamentalist
- Follower
- Literalist

PEOPLE: John Lennon, Pablo Picasso, Michael Jackson, George Orwell

FOR BRANDS THAT: enable their customers to create

BRANDS: Lego, YouTube, iPad, Crayola, Nikon, Paper-Source, Photoshop, 3M

THE EMPEROR

The Emperor is the boss, the chief, king of the castle, the *capo di tutti capi*. He exudes power and exerts leadership and dominance over others. He prefers products that offer an opportunity to stand above the crowd, whether in price, quality, service, or performance.

SAYINGS AN EMPEROR MIGHT LIVE BY:

- "It's good to be king."
- "Rise above the crowd."
- "Being number one is its own reward."

CHAMPIONS VALUES SUCH AS:

Leadership, Strength, Determination, Influence, Respect, Dominance, Prosperity, Confidence, Control, Wealth

DISDAINS:

- Losing
- Chaos
- Being Poor
- Lowliness
- Shoddiness

OPPOSITES:

- Submissiveness
- Powerlessness
- Inconsequence
- Subservience
- Following
- Laziness
- Weakness

PEOPLE: Bill Gates, Donald Trump, Michael Bloomberg, Warren Buffet, Mark Zuckerberg, Margaret Thatcher, Hillary Clinton

FOR BRANDS THAT:

denote power and help build customers' leadership and superiority

BRANDS:

Porsche, The Peninsula, American Express, Cartier, Chanel, Johnnie Walker Blue, The Robb Report, Rolex, Tiffany, The Four Seasons, Cadillac

THE REBEL

The Rebel is unsatisfied with the status quo and abhors convention. His behavior may be disruptive or even shocking and outrageous to some, but to others he represents someone who will do whatever it takes to protect his self-expression.

SAYINGS A REBEL MIGHT LIVE BY:

- "Born free."
- "Rules are meant to be broken."
- "Take the road less traveled."

CHAMPIONS VALUES SUCH AS:

Freedom, Nonconformity, Independence, Individuality, Controversy, Rebellion, Daringness, Boldness, Defiance

DISDAINS:

- Powerlessness
- Loss of Identity

OPPOSITES:

- Group-think
- Dependence
- Passiveness
- Conformity
- Timidity
- Cowardice

PEOPLE: Howard Stern, Dennis Rodman, Quentin Tarantino, Lady Gaga, James Dean

FOR BRANDS THAT:

rebel against convention, take chances, and pride themselves on their individuality

BRANDS:

Harley-Davidson, Red Bull, GoDaddy, Converse, X Games, World Wrestling Entertainment, Inc. (WWE)

THE SOURCE

The Source is looked upon as the all-knowing provider of knowledge. He devours information in the pursuit of knowledge and expertise. He has a high level of curiosity and is looked to for advice and opinions.

SAYINGS A SOURCE MIGHT LIVE BY:

- "We owe it to ourselves to find the truth."
- "Knowledge is power."

CHAMPIONS VALUES SUCH AS:

Truth, Knowledge, Expertise, Intelligence, Rigor, Diligence, Objectivity, Commitment, Depth, Education, Discipline, Clarity

DISDAINS:

- Uncertainty
- Deception
- Falsehood

OPPOSITES:

- Impetuousness
- Irrationality
- Naiveté
- Ignorance
- Treachery
- Bias
- Dishonesty

PEOPLE: Oprah Winfrey, Dr. Phil, Albert Einstein

FOR BRANDS THAT:

are looked upon for trusted advice, knowledge, or specialized expertise

BRANDS:

Harvard, Bloomberg, McKinsey, Forrester, Wall Street Journal

THE STRAIGHT SHOOTER

The Straight Shooter abhors pretension and is no-nonsense. He will say it like it is and behave in ways he believes are true to himself. He values being real in all that he does and in his relationships with others. He's friendly and informal. He's not one to keep up with the Joneses and marches to the beat of his own voice.

SAYINGS A STRAIGHT SHOOTER MIGHT LIVE BY:

- "I am who I am."
- "Be true to yourself."
- "Tell it like it is."

CHAMPIONS VALUES SUCH AS:

Realism, Authenticity, Honesty, Modesty, Frankness

DISDAINS:

- Faking it
- Self-Delusion
- Deceit

OPPOSITES:

- Pretension
- Superficiality
- Arrogance

PEOPLE: Andre Agassi, Simon Cowell, Whoopi Goldberg, Charles Barkley

FOR BRANDS THAT:

are common and everyday—they tell it like it is and promote function over form or style

BRANDS:

Levi's, Miller Beer, Southwest Airlines, Wrangler Jeans, Jim Beam

APPLYING ARCHETYPES

Using archetypes to describe the character of the brand story is an extremely helpful way to start articulating motivations, perceptions, likes, dislikes, and a whole host of psychological traits that explain behavior. In that way, we become immersed in the brand as a person, the hero of our story.

Our process for arriving at archetypes differs from what is prescribed by the Mark/Pearson model. We do not adhere to the same strict guidelines that require a selection of one and only one archetype that represents the brand. We do, however, wholeheartedly support their notion that it is important to characterize a brand in a simple, easy-to-comprehend, memorable way. And we are well aware of studies that have been conducted showing how blending or compromising archetypes adds to brand identity confusion. However, we believe that a rigid adherence to this or any given list of archetypes, no matter how well researched, will limit one's ability to find inner-layer uniqueness vs. competing brands.

From the twelve archetypes above, we divide them into two piles. The first pile consists of what we are or could be. The second pile consists of archetypes that are way outside the realm of possibilities. At this stage in developing the brand story, it is premature to land on an archetypal description of the brand. It is more advisable to wait until the third C, characterizing the prospect, for that.

With that said, however, I need to point out an important caveat with archetypal analysis. Our main objective in using archetypes is to provide a useful frame of reference when referring to brand values and beliefs. Our objective is not, I repeat NOT to arrive at a rigid archetypal description of the brand from the twelve archetypes that we have chosen to use. Archetypes should be used as an aid to judgment.

Striving to become as single-minded as possible is necessary.

However, deciding on one archetype as described in our definitions of that archetype can lead to big mistakes. It is important to allow for flexibility, understanding that each archetype described has variations and nuances. Furthermore, archetypes can blend into each other; their borders are not firm and impenetrable. It is better to think of a brand as LIKE a hero, and/or LIKE a magician, than to decide whether or not there is a hand-in-glove fit between a given brand and a particular archetype. It is perfectly okay (and we've done it ourselves on many occasions) to invent an archetypal description that is not included in the twelve we have described. Again, avoid seeing these twelve archetypes as hard-and-fast brand descriptors. Rather, see them as providing guidelines that will, if allowed, enhance productive and insightful discussions about the brand's inner layer. Archetypal analysis is a means to an end and not an end in itself.

FINAL THOUGHTS ON YOUR BRAND'S INNER LAYER

One of the most important acknowledgments we make using the Story-Branding process is that brands are more complex than what they appear to be on the surface, which is often limited to advantage and benefit descriptions. I'm often asked if the brand's inner layer is the same as the brand's *personality* or *essence*. Those two terms mean different things to different people, so I can't compare and contrast. Regardless of what it's compared to, the brand's inner layer, stripped down to its core and plainly stated, is the body of values and beliefs that a brand stands for and is associated with. To achieve a Level IV connection with the prospect, shared brand–prospect values must come into play, the same way shared values define our closest relationships with people.

Archetypal analysis is a diagnostic tool for the purpose of aiding judgment. It is not an exact science and does not purport to be. Its main purpose is to provide a common language that helps us relate to the brand as a person. By studying, comparing, and contrasting brands in this way, it is much easier to identify a brand's value system.

If you're interested in reading more about archetypes and how they are applied to branding, I recommend *Literature and Film as Modern Mythology* by William K. Ferrell.

Review

- The goal of archetypal analysis is to give us the language, the frames of reference, that we need to bring the brand's meaning out of hiding.

- Thinking of the brand as a person, we use archetypes to analyze a brand's inner layer, or the driving force behind why it does what it does, beyond the profit motive.

- Wikipedia describes an archetype as "an original model of a person, ideal example, or a prototype after which others are copied, patterned, or emulated; a symbol universally recognized by all."

- If an archetype is to be invented from a combination or blending of different archetypes, it needs to be described in not more than two words, e.g., the creative-maverick or the hero-joker.

- Archetypal analysis is a means to an end and not an end in itself.

CHAPTER 11

The Brand's Outer Layer

*Companies have to wake up to the fact that they are more
than a product on a shelf. They're behavior as well.*
—Robert Haas, Levi Strauss

The brand's inner and outer layers are akin to themes and plots in stories. As we've discussed, story themes, like the brand's inner layer, consist of a deeper purpose. Themes provide the means through which the author or the brand supplies meaning. The plot, like the brand's outer layer, explains the *how*. For stories, plots tell how the character deals with certain obstacles to achieve some goal. For brands, the outer layer explains how the product that is associated with the brand functions to help the prospect deal with certain obstacles in order achieve to some goal.

A constant debate among story writers is whether to start with the plot or the theme. The *plotters* believe that one should just start with the plot and see where things go. According to them, the theme will just naturally reveal itself. The *themers*, on the other hand, believe that one should identify the purpose of the story first and build the plot around it.

This is to make certain that intention never gets lost. Either way, plot and theme need to be balanced. A great plot with an insignificant message is mere entertainment and probably soon forgotten. A great message with a boring plot may never get the attention it needs to resonate.

But one has to start somewhere. And when it comes to developing brand stories, and especially for mature brands, we subscribe to the *themers'* point of view. As we've suggested earlier, when all is said and done, the brand's inner layer is ultimately more important to achieving a Level IV connection. For established brands, the outer layer or how the associated product solves a certain problem can provide important clues as to what the brand's theme is. But a brand's outer layer should be seen as a function of the brand and not the brand itself. Furthermore, as stated earlier, you can count on the fact that your outer layer will be copied or outdone by some innovation sooner or later. On the other hand, your brand's inner layer, or what it stands for and represents, can last forever. And since inner layers are emotionally charged, they are more responsible for the brand's overall magnetism.

While analyzing the brand's inner layer, you've no doubt discovered a number of different themes with which your brand can be readily associated. We are now at the stage where it is important to consider *how* these values and beliefs would manifest themselves through product features and benefits. If your brand is The Imagineer, how does that get revealed through your products? If you are The Protector, then how do a product's features and benefits serve as proof? Contrary to what is often prescribed, we believe that the outer layer's purpose is to serve the inner layer, not vice versa. Certainly the purpose of the outer layer is to show the prospect how the brand can solve problems. But a more important purpose is to support or validate the brand's meaning.

For instance, The Ritz Hotel can be described by The King archetype. It has long been known for being the hotel where "ladies and gentlemen should serve ladies and gentlemen." The values of success and elitism are celebrated there. The theme of their story stems from the belief that accomplished people deserve service that goes beyond the ordinary. How does this manifest itself? That's where the brand's outer layer goes to work. The Ritz demonstrates this belief by employing four people for every guest, by allowing employees to spend up to $2,000 a year to satisfy a single guest, and by making sure that, from the moment you pull up your car until the time you leave, you are treated like a rock star. These features and benefits serve as proof of The Ritz's inner layer.

We often see marketers getting their inner layer (theme) mixed up with their outer layer (plot). Actually, this problem is quite prevalent. When we first interview new or prospective clients, one of the first questions we ask is, "What makes your brand significant?" What we're digging for is often referred to as an "elevator pitch." Invariably, we get an answer that is the domain of the outer layer, e.g., "Our restaurants specialize in providing food with unique tastes and textures," or "We're the biggest network of health clubs in the United States," or "Our casinos have the loosest slots."

Marketers often refer to their specialness in very concrete, rational terms. Describing the brand this way is like describing its body, without regard for its soul. One of the reasons why the question of uniqueness is relegated to the brand's outer layer has to do with our training. Since the days of Rosser Reeves, once considered the father of modern advertising, marketers have been taught to describe brand differences functionally and rationally in terms of what Reeves described as a brand's unique selling proposition or USP. Unfortunately, this is usually linked to something the brand does as opposed to what it means. And, as we discussed in the last chapter, the hero's behavior is not nearly as important as his or her motivation.

After years of asking clients to tell us about their USPs or give us their elevator pitches, I came to the realization that most of them stink. But then, I also came to the realization that my question stinks as well. If one is looking for a description of the inner layer, this is not the way to get it. The inner layer can be pretty squishy and difficult to articulate concretely. I myself have yet to come up with an elevator pitch that I can use at cocktail parties, networking events, or other places where they are supposed to come in handy. Expressed in terms of our inner layer, it would go something like this: "We believe in the persuasive power of story." And with that, I might clear a room. So I, like everyone else, resort to talking about our outer layer: "We are a full-service marketing communications agency that does *blah blah* and for clients like *blah, blah,* and *blah*." And while I'm saying this, I know that this is hardly what makes us special. Moreover, it is not enough to get us to a Level IV connection with prospects.

Thus, I've learned to accept any answer I'm given to the question about what makes a brand special, different, or distinctive. But I steadfastly adhere to the notion that meaning cannot be found in plots. It can only be found through themes.

Consider the following story:

The boy went to the store to buy some milk. When he walked in, he saw a burglar holding up the cashier. He quickly ran out of the store.

Meaningful? Compare it to this one:

The young man went to the store. When he walked in he saw a burglar holding up the cashier. Panicked, he ran as fast as he could out the front door to his car. The next day as he read the local paper's headline, "Store Cashier Shot by Burglar," he thought he should call the police to tell them what he knew. Years later, looking back on a life unfulfilled, he cannot escape why he didn't make that call.

Both of these stories provide plots or a chain of events that occurred. But the latter provides a more important reason for the story to be told.

And whether or not it's a story that hits home, it's one that we can empathize with simply because it illustrates our own potential.

The first story is similar to the type of advertising we see day in and day out: ads with an overemphasis on superlatives. They parade wall-to-wall features and benefits, many of them ending in -*st*, as in best, fastest, or biggest, in front of viewers, and then an irrelevant theme is thrown in at the end. But more often than not, the so-called theme is more of a plot line because it implies something the brand does, as opposed to a value the brand stands for. I will discuss themes more fully in Part III when the subject becomes how to tell the brand story, once it is planned.

THE YIN AND THE YANG OF THEMES AND PLOTS

Annette Simmons, author of *The Story Factor: Inspiration, Influence, and Persuasion Through the Art of Storytelling* and one of the foremost experts on the power of story, writes: "[People] are up to their eyeballs in information. They want faith—faith in you. It is faith that moves mountains, that inspires belief in you, and renews hope that your ideas indeed offer what you promise."

When it comes to faith, again, don't just sell the church. Sell the religion.

This is not to suggest that factual information, to which she refers, is unimportant. Quite the contrary. A story can't be all theme without a plot. Similarly, all plot and no theme makes for a meaningless, soon-to-be-insignificant story. As mentioned, it's a matter of finding the appropriate balance. Deciding the importance of the brand's outer layer relative to its inner layer is always a matter of judgment. However, here are some guidelines we use when facts are especially important:

1. **New news:** When a brand is being introduced, and especially when it provides a discernible and dramatic functional

difference, then it only makes sense to emphasize features and benefits. When a functional feature or benefit is new and important, then facts should be flaunted. Remember, in order to get to a Level IV connection, the lower levels have to be achieved first.

However, do not stop here. This is not where real connections with the prospect are made. Again, today's news is tomorrow's history. If a brand is solely dependent on new product news to sustain it, obsolescence will take place sooner or later as competitive substitutes start shouting "me too." Furthermore, keeping the brand new is expensive, as additional outlays for R&D, packaging, advertising, operations, and a host of other marketing variables have to be reinvented. As I've said throughout this book, the ultimate goal for every brand should be to achieve a Level IV connection with the prospect. There is never a safe harbor from competitive activity, but once the prospect is affiliated with the brand such that the brand represents some important value shared by the prospect, some protection is attained.

No matter how innovative HP becomes, an Apple user is relatively committed to the Apple brand. No matter how proven the claim that a Cleveland driver can outdistance other golf drivers, a Calloway user will find it hard to part with his Calloway. To get to Level IV, something must emotionally resonate with the prospect, with or without new facts or product superiority claims.

2. **When price is important:** When price is discernibly better than your competitor's, talk it up. However if price is all you've got, you will face serious problems unless you can sustain high volume to overcome constant discounting. Price superiority is usually a better short-term tactic than a long-term strategy.

3. **When risks are high:** Deciding between the purchase of a Cessna or a Grumman jet will no doubt require a prospect to survey more facts than will deciding between Fritos regular or barbeque chips. Nevertheless, it's important to know that even high-risk brands can't survive on facts alone for too long. Facts become less important as brand meaning becomes something that the prospect wants to associate with.

    A high-risk brand choice that we are faced with every four years is the election or reelection of our president. Political advisers know that elections are won or lost on their ability to sway voters who have little allegiance to one party or another. Numerous studies have shown that party affiliation is declining. But still, for the majority of voters, party values have more to do with their choices than does a candidate's stance on specific issues. Can a Democrat be swayed to vote Republican and vice versa? It happens all the time. But what occurs most often is a vote along party lines because of the all-encompassing inner-layer values associated with the differing philosophies of these two parties.

THE OUTER LAYER IS THE CONFIDENCE BUILDER

Whereas defining the brand's inner layer is clearly one of the main messages of this book, knowing this does not limit the need to promote the functional satisfaction that the outer layer provides. But it does put the brand's outer layer in proper perspective. The outer layer's role is not primary; it is supportive. It builds confidence in the brand so that the gate can be opened to a Level III and Level IV connection. Without confidence in how well a product will perform, there is no basis for a brand–prospect relationship to exist, no matter what the brand stands for or believes in. Brand connections are achieved to the extent that the outer layer keeps the prospect believing in the inner layer. Just as a brand will break down when the inner layer is hollow or meaningless, it will certainly perish to the extent that there is no outer support for or congruity with the brand's inner layer. Therefore, the outer layer's role should not be taken lightly. It must consistently be the walk of the brand's talk. Especially in today's marketplace, brand confidence is becoming harder to achieve.

As consumers of advertising, we have all come a long way since the early days of TV. Advertising has never been completely trusted. But over time it has significantly lost trust.

While gazing upon my two young grandkids watching a McDonald's TV commercial, the three-year-old said to the five-year-old, "Why do they say they love to make you smile? They don't make me smile."

And the five-year-old replied, "Because it's advertising, stupid."

Distrust of advertising now starts at a very early age. We have grown to become suspicious of advertising. As shown in a number of Gallup polls conducted in recent years, advertisers rank one notch above used-car salesmen when it comes to having high standards. And judging from my grandson, that trend isn't going to change with the next generation. Back in the day when TV advertising was relatively new, source credibility was more readily granted. Just being big and successful enough to advertise on TV was enough to establish trust. It's clear that much has changed. Furthermore, technology has become advertising's kryptonite, allowing people to avoid what was once forced upon them. Today, try as they might, advertisers cannot simply make claims about their outer layers and assume this will gain confidence with prospects. Source credibility is no longer freely granted. It has to be earned. And given the ubiquity of chat rooms, forums, and Internet reviews, we're getting to the point where what the advertiser claims as true or factual doesn't matter.

Not too long ago, Walmart was found to be *flogging*, or posting fake blogs. A blog ostensibly authored by a couple traveling across America in their RV and spending nights parked in Walmart parking lots turned out to be sourced by, you guessed it, Walmart. Consequently, Walmart's "good guy" authenticity was called into question.

Inner and outer layer incongruities always make for attention-grabbing headlines. But it can sometimes become the subject of entire books. In his book *The Coke Machine: The Dirty Truth Behind the World's Favorite Soft Drink*, Michael Landing takes the quintessential all-American beverage to task for anti-union activities in South America, activities that have resulted in the deaths of union activists. Politicians, athletes, and celebrities provide many examples of how inner-layer values can be undermined. One of the most famous cases is the Tiger Woods scandal that forced some marketers, who had paid dearly for his endorsement, to dismiss him from their payrolls. He clearly was not the Purist-Emperor we thought he was.

Hypocrisy can kill a brand. Brands must shield themselves from falsity at all costs. Furthermore, the brand's inner layer must (not just should) be substantiated through all the brand's touch points to be perceived as true to its principles. Advertising is certainly one of the most visible touch points. But ultimately, what we often refer to as *The Moment of Truth* reveals itself during the interaction between customers and the people representing the brand. How a customer gets treated is the ultimate test of a brand's veracity. Too often, marketing and operations people work along different paths when it comes to service delivery. Everything the customer sees and experiences must come together as harmonious proof that the brand walks its talk.

One of the oft-used examples of outer-layer and inner-layer alignment is exemplified by Zappos, an online shoe and clothing retailer. But they are much more than your run-of-the-mill e-tailer. Zappos has a service culture like few others in the country. I went on a tour of their headquarters in Henderson, Nevada, to experience their brand behavior for myself. What I experienced was a company that lives and breathes the belief that companies should be driven by a no-holds-barred desire to deliver happiness to both customers and employees. In an interview with *Bloomberg Businessweek*, Tony Hsieh, Zappos CEO, is quoted as saying, "Whether it's the happiness our customers receive when they get a new pair of shoes or the perfect piece of clothing, or the happiness they get when dealing with a friendly customer rep over the phone, or the happiness our employees feel about being a part of a culture that celebrates their individuality, these are all ways we bring happiness to people's lives."[*] This belief manifests itself in a 365-day, no-questions-asked return policy, free surprise overnight shipping for most customers, and a standing offer to call about anything. And when you talk with a Zappos rep, it's likely that you'll get a handwritten thank-you card soon after your order arrives.

Zappos employees are empowered to deliver the Protector's promise of happiness. To retain people who truly want to be part of the Zappos service culture, there is a standing offer of $2,000 to anyone who decides to leave the company for any reason. And each year, Zappos publishes a *culture book* that includes statements from each and every employee on anything (uncensored) about their experience working at Zappos. Their culture book also includes pictures and descriptions of ongoing employee events that keep their happy environment alive.

Another company that actively makes certain its outer and inner layers are congruent is Cosi Restaurants. Cosi is a regional, fast-casual restaurant chain with locations throughout the Midwest and the East Coast. When a new employee is hired, he or she is referred to as a partner

---

[*] Carmine Gallo, "Delivering Happiness the Zappos Way," *Bloomberg Businessweek*, May 12, 2009.

and made to feel that way. Employees are trained in Cosi's customer-centric service methods, and they learn about the unique nature of their clientele and their high regard for Cosi's service ethic. They learn that they are an extension of their brand's theme that *Life should be delicious.* Additionally, Cosi is very careful to hire only those people who can demonstrate a passion for delivering their notable service. Whether their job is greeting the customer with a genuine, "Hey, how you doin' today," baking bread to perfection, or answering mundane questions, employees are continuously supported by management, all the way to the top of the organization. Their CEO is often seen in Cosi's restaurants walking the talk and remembering every partner's name. In addition to a constantly updated menu that appeals to the global palate of Cosi's clientele, the company's service ethic embraces the idea that everything about Cosi should live up to its belief that a restaurant should provide an exploratory experience in addition to delicious food.

The value of authenticity increases as we become more apt to separate fact from fiction. As we become more sophisticated in our knowledge of things, our BS antennae have become more sensitive. Today there can be no hiding the truth about the brand underneath the cloak of what it promotes itself to be.

ACHIEVING ALIGNMENT

If one of your brand's archetypes is the Imagineer, then to support it you must be able to dramatize beauty and celebrate your imaginative products. If you see that your brand can be like the Conqueror, then ultimately you must be able to demonstrate achievement or explain how your product can help prospects achieve. The outer layer should empirically support the belief that you want prospects to associate with your brand.

When there is misalignment, as in the case of hypocrisy or irrelevance, then consumers will naturally withdraw faith in what your brand stands for. It would be totally incongruous for Harley-Davidson, the Maverick, to conduct a sweepstakes for free trips to Disney World. Likewise, it would be incongruous for Disney World to provide discount coupons for Victoria's Secret. These are extreme examples, but each time the inner and outer layers are out of sync, the inner layer is obscured and the brand-prospect link is weakened. Conversely, each time the inner layer and the outer layer mesh, the consumer's faith in the brand hero is strengthened.

NEXT STEP

If you've identified a number of different archetypes to describe your brand, now substantiate each of them. Think of features and benefits that can now or will in the future prove the authenticity of what the brand stands for. You might be tempted to eliminate some of the archetypes at this stage if they're weak. I strongly advise you not to eliminate anything from consideration until you get to Step 3, where we'll discuss matching brand and prospect inner and outer layers.

Review

- The brand's inner layer works much like the theme or heart of a story. It is where meaning resides. The outer layer is the plot or what we sometimes refer to as the *how so* of the brand.

- The outer layer consists of the facts that support the inner layer. Marketers often refer to their specialness in concrete, rational terms. Describing the brand this way is like describing its body, without regard for its soul.

- Benefits should not be seen as one-time affairs. Rather they should enhance other benefits that together support the brand's inner layer.

- A story can't be all theme and no plot. But all plot and no theme make for a meaningless story. It's merely a matter of finding the appropriate balance.

- The outer layer's role is not primary; it is supportive. It builds confidence in the brand so that the gate can be opened to a Level IV brand affiliation.

- Source credibility is no longer freely granted. It has to be earned.

- Hypocrisy can kill a brand. Brands must shield themselves from falsity at all cost.

- When there is incongruity, as in the case of hypocrisy or irrelevance, then consumers will naturally withdraw faith in what your brand stands for.

- The value of authenticity increases as we become more apt to separate fact from fiction.

CHAPTER 12

The Prospect's Layers

*Great stories agree with our world view. The best stories don't
teach people anything new. Instead, the best stories agree with what
the audience already believes and makes the members of the audience feel
smart and secure when reminded how right they were in the first place.*
—Seth Godin, *Tribes: We Need You to Lead Us*

By now you are familiar with the difference between an outer layer and
an inner layer. The same concept is applied to the prospect's character.
Consequently, less explanation of layers is needed here. So instead of having separate chapters dedicated to each individual layer the way we discussed the brand character in chapters 8 and 9, they are combined here.

DIFFERENCES BETWEEN THE PROSPECT'S OUTER AND INNER LAYERS

A prospect's outer layer is what we often describe as the flat definition
of the prospect. If a writer wants to achieve a higher degree of empathy

for a given character, he or she will need to round out that character by giving it some depth. To do this, just as a writer would, we excavate the inner layer of our brand. Unfortunately, brand or creative briefs, if they allow for this excavation, do so in an oversimplified way in which key insights are either glossed over or ignored altogether. Taking the lead from storytellers, we spend a great deal of time fleshing out the beliefs and values that will eventually lead to a Level IV connection between the brand and the prospect (or the character and the reader, in our analogy).

The inner layer consists of relevant ideas and values that are important to the prospect. Whereas the outer layer deals with what the functional need is, the inner layer explains why that need is important. Given our goal of achieving a strong relationship with the prospect, it's vital to know what the inner layer is. Whether in stories or in real life, shared values are the foundation of strong relationships. The number and importance of shared values account for the difference between acquaintanceships and friendships. We all have acquaintances who share our interests in sports, music, movies, politics, bingo, or other activities. However, the people we truly bond with are those with whom we share ideas about what is truly important in life. I enjoy getting together with my buddies on weekends to swap the vicissitudes of life for the vicissitudes of the golf course. But among these buddies, my truest friends are those who have a similar outlook on life, similar priorities, and value other things more than lowering their golf handicap.

EXAMINING THE PROSPECT THROUGH LADDERING

When examining the prospect, we sometimes start with the outer layer and work back toward the inner layer. One technique that helps us do this is called laddering.

Sometimes referred to as means-end chain analysis, laddering is a research technique developed by two college professors, Thomas Reynolds and Jonathan Gutman. Essentially, laddering is used to explore both outer-layer reasons and their associated inner-layer beliefs for desired features and benefits. Personal interviews (called one-on-ones) are conducted to arrive at hierarchical structures of *cognitive ladders*. These ladders reflect the way we think about a given product or service.

The laddering interview begins with a simple question, and then another question is asked about that response.

Interviewer: "Why x?"

Subject: "Because z."

Interviewer: "Why z?"

Subject: "Because b."

Interviewer: "Why b?"

For purposes of illustration, say we're studying a brand of laundry detergent called Bleach Bright. And one of the most important attributes cited is bleach crystals that have been shown to increase brightness 15 percent more than the leading laundry detergent can. Here's how a typical laddering interview might continue from that point:

Moderator: You said that bleach crystals are important when you're considering laundry detergent. Why is that?

Respondent: Because they ensure that the whites will be white, in fact 15 percent brighter than leading laundry detergents.

Moderator: Why is that important?

Respondent: Because if the clothes don't come out white, they look dirty.

Moderator: Why is that important?

Respondent: Because I don't want my kids looking like they are wearing dirty clothes.

Moderator: Why is that important?

Respondent: Well, I don't want people to think that I'm the kind of mother who would let her kids wear dirty clothes.

Moderator: Why is that important?

Respondent: Because I'm not that kind of mother.

Moderator: Why is it important for others to know you're not that kind of mother?

Respondent: Because I think I should get credit for the kind of mother I really am.

Moderator: Why is that important?

Respondent: Recognition, I guess.

Moderator: What do you get out of feeling recognized as a good mother?

Respondent: It makes me feel good about myself.

More often than not, self-esteem is the last rung of every ladder and is usually where the probing stops.

The ladder that we constructed with the aid of the prospect helps us define both of the prospect's layers. To this respondent, white clothes are clearly very important. This helps define the functional need that is part of this prospect's outer layer. This functional need is associated with the emotional need to feel good about her role as a mother. For her, seeing her kids in white clothes both avoids guilt and enhances recognition for being the kind of mother she thinks she should be. To another person it might be that white clothes enhance confidence. Her reasons for needing white clothes may have something to do with the notion that bright white clothes help her to feel sure of herself while assuaging self-consciousness. In either case, laddering uncovers both problems and opportunities that a brand can address, both rationally and emotionally.

By looking at the various ladders and drawing from the demographics of respondents, we might be able to determine who the most likely
prospects are, especially when the pattern of responses is consistent.
On the other hand, we may find that different outer- and inner-layer
segments exist. When we get to Step 4 and start looking for matches
between the brand and the prospect, we will be in a better position to
determine which of those segments presents the best opportunity for
the brand to promote or target.

OTHER TECHNIQUES USED TO DEFINE THE PROSPECT

Two other types of techniques can be used to get at the prospect's outer
and inner layers. The first consists of a large body of projective techniques.
The second consists of what some refer to as ethnographic research.

Projective Techniques

Unless you are relying on a trained interviewer, it may be difficult or
impossible to get a respondent to articulate his or her reasons for needing
or wanting certain benefits, both functional and emotional. Projective
research can be used instead. This draws from a large body of different techniques, all of which provide prompts (or stimuli) to encourage
respondents to project their underlying motivations, beliefs, attitudes, or
feelings onto an ambiguous situation.
Examples of projective techniques include

- Word association: The respondent says the first word that comes to
  mind after hearing a certain word and is asked to word-associate
  with competitive brands, such as Lexus, BMW, and Mercedes, to
  see what different words are used to describe them.

- Sentence completion: Respondents are given incomplete sentences and asked to complete them. For example, a sentence may begin, the biggest problem I have with my dishwasher is _____. Or, the best dishwashers are those that _____. Or, I wish I had a dishwasher that _____.

- Story completion: Respondents are given part of a story and are asked to complete it. For example, John and Mary are getting married. John feels that it is important to_____ because _____. Or, one of Bob's neighbors just bought a new lawn mower. Bob is somewhat envious because it is made by_____.

- Cartoon tests: Respondents are shown cartoon characters in a specific situation and with dialogue balloons. One of the balloons is empty, and the respondent is asked to fill it in. For example, a woman is shown looking at purses in a Gucci store. There's a thought bubble above her head. The respondent is asked to fill it in with what the woman might be saying to herself.

- Role playing: Respondents are asked to play the role of someone else. For example, a respondent might be asked to be an insurance salesman. It is assumed that the respondent will project his or her feelings about what to expect from insurance salesmen.

Whatever technique is used, insights can be gained about the respondents' functional and emotional needs.

Ethnographic Research

Ethnographic techniques are currently in vogue as a means to excavate both the outer and inner layer of prospects. These have roots in techniques used by anthropologists when they observe tribes, cultures, or societies. Direct observation is used to discern prospects' wants, needs, and underlying motivations.

Electrolux is a company that has benefited from ethnographic research. Instead of using marketing surveys, Electrolux regularly observes the way appliances are used in the homes of potential prospects. In one case, Electrolux was able to discern that bottled water was being purchased regularly but was using up valuable storage space. Furthermore, the assortment of refrigerators on the market that provided filtered water did so from inlets that took up too much of the refrigerators' space capacity. With this insight, Electrolux created a refrigerator that supplied filtered water and ice from a compact inlet, which also satisfied the prospect's need for tapping into the benefits of bottled water.

In another case, they were able to see that households with one or two people were using large, inefficient dishwashers. Dishes were washed once or twice a week, which meant that coffee cups or other frequently used dishes weren't being cleaned every day. To meet this need, Electrolux invented a dishwasher the size of a large microwave oven that could be readily used on a daily basis.

Not only was Electrolux able to discern unmet functional needs by using ethnographic research, but it also associated itself with the inner-layer value of providing unexpected solutions to everyday problems.

SUMMARY

At this point, you should have some idea of both the brand's and the prospect's potential inner and outer layers. In the crucial next step, we will explore ways in which we can arrive at an optimal matching of both what the brand can and should provide that will establish a strong and enduring relationship with the prospect.

Review

- Simply stated, the prospect's outer layer is found in the answer to two questions: What does the prospect look like? What is the prospect's problem that the functional advantages and benefits of the brand will solve?

- The outer layer of a prospect is what authors might refer to as a flat character. To achieve a higher degree of empathy, we have to convert this character into a round one.

- Whereas the outer layer deals with the functional need, the inner layer explains why that need is important. Whether in stories or in real life, shared values are the foundation of strong relationships. An oft-used research technique that can help identify both outer-layer functional needs and corresponding inner-layer values is a qualitative technique called laddering.

- The purpose of laddering is to arrive at underlying beliefs that explain why people behave the way they do.

- Projective techniques and ethnographic research can also be employed to arrive at insights about the prospect's buying behaviors.

CHAPTER 13

Finding the Right Match

If you will, pretend for a moment that you have been asked to write a story—not a brand story, a story story. Using story structure you are aware that a story consists of a character dealing with an obstacle to achieve some goal. Take out the obstacle for a moment and consider the character-goal combinations you could write about. The character could be a bank robber setting out to conduct a major bank heist. It could be a spy trying to gather important government intelligence or a musician trying to become recognized for his or her talent. For every character you come up with, given their expected role, there will be an appropriate and logical connection between them and their goals. In the case of the bank robber, for instance, the logical goal would be to steal money, not to gather government intelligence or to gain fame for his or her musical talents.

This bank robber character/goal matchup may seem obvious, but when it comes to brand stories, matching the brand with an appropriate marketing goal is where things can go awry. Consider *Cosmopolitan* magazine when it tried to sell yogurt as an extension of the *Cosmopolitan* brand. Or Smith & Wesson—yes, the maker of guns—when they marketed the Smith & Wesson bicycle.

Certainly these examples of mismatches are extreme, but some seem to make sense yet fail for less obvious reasons. Take Life Savers, the #1 brand of non-chocolate candies. They once branded a soft drink that fared well in taste tests. However, it failed miserably because prospects thought they would be drinking liquid candy. Numerous case studies exhibit a brand extension that was flawed from the start because of a perceived discrepancy between the brand's expected role and its new goal.

For any brand, the ideal match is one where the brand's and the prospect's inner- and outer-layer cells are in alignment. For instance, the brand's outer-layer functional solution should be perceived as a relevant fit with the prospect's outer-layer functional problem. Additionally, values and beliefs of both characters' inner layers should match up as well. Where mismatches exist, problems will also, sometimes too difficult to overcome.

In Step 2 of the StoryBranding process, we outlined a few ways in which the brand could be described archetypally in terms of where it is now and/or where it ideally wants to be. We also considered a number of perceived functional benefits that could be associated with the brand's outer layer. In Step 3, and separate from our analysis of the brand, we looked both at and into the prospect's functional needs and motivations. We looked at possible functional needs in search of a solution, and we considered emotional needs as well. Moving into Step 4, what we have now is a salad bar dilemma. Faced with different combinations and permutations between possible brand–prospect matchups, the challenge is to walk away with the best complements while avoiding a mixture of green peas with pineapples. The simplicity or complexity of this challenge is completely dependent upon the number of brand and prospect alternatives considered viable.

For the purpose of clarity, it is advisable to construct outer- and inner-layer combinations for each character showing outer- and inner-layer relationships. Once completed, look for matches between the characters. Using the Bleach Bright example discussed earlier, you might end up with something similar to the illustration on the next page.

Of course, given this hypothetical situation, a number of assumptions have been made that might or might not be true. First it is assumed that the primary purchasers of laundry detergent are women who are eighteen years of age or older. It is also assumed that, while considering the prospect's inner layer and as shown in the three circles, three values were identified for three separate segments without the help of any research. Quite possibly other segments and other values could have been identified.

But assuming that, following Step 2, we ended up here, we see three distinct possibilities for the brand story. Let's refer to them as: 1) Brand as Protector; 2) Brand as Emperor; and 3) Brand as Wizard. To arrive at the best story, and to help eliminate risk, we look at each against two criteria: (1) the quantity of the opportunity and (2) the quality of the opportunity.

THE QUANTITY OF THE OPPORTUNITY

The quantity of the opportunity is nothing more than a measure of the potential size of the market. It is usually the easiest to arrive at since the answer is in numbers that can be readily obtained. Clearly in this case, for instance, the numbers are more in favor of Wizard than they are for the other two stories because we've assumed that the universe is all women, regardless of their roles as mothers or workers.

The Brand

The Prospect

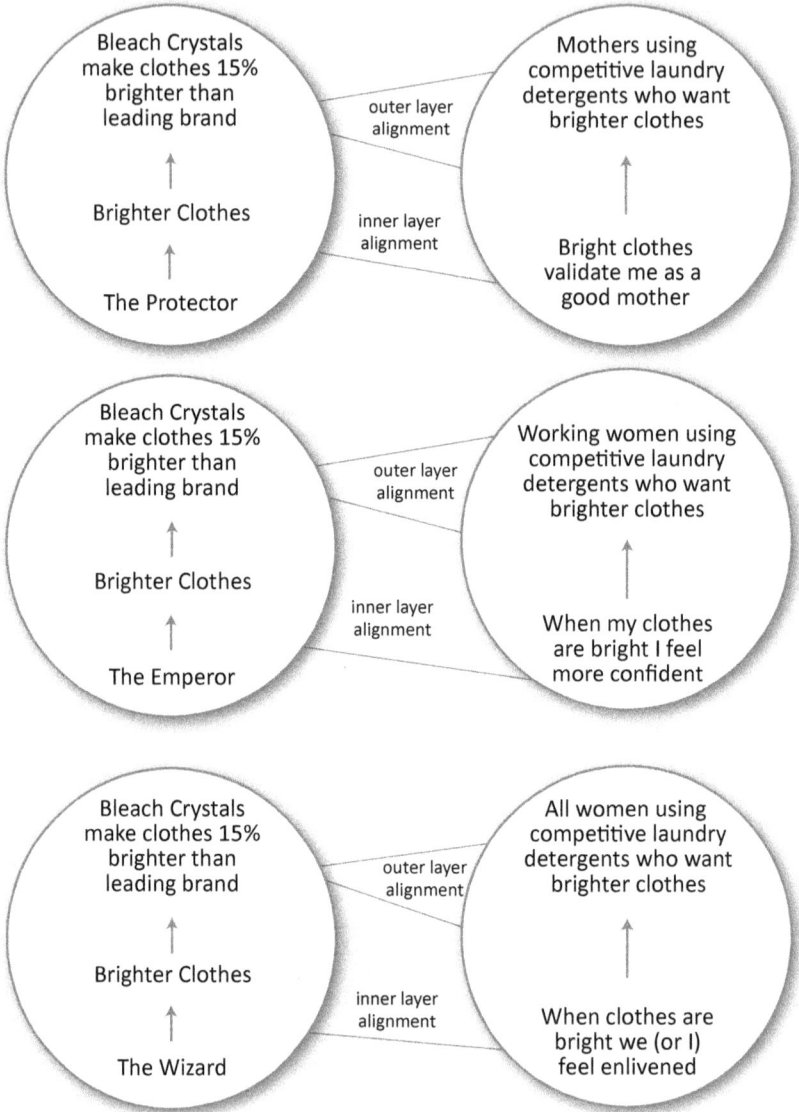

THE QUALITY OF THE OPPORTUNITY

The quality of the opportunity has to do with the ease of persuasion. How likely is it going to be that the outer/inner layer brand combination will fit the outer/inner layer prospect combination in each case? In some cases, it might be plain to see. My experience, however, is that in most cases some research is required, especially for instances where a major sum of money is at stake. The research can be conducted in a number of ways, and an equal number of pros and cons can be associated with each research technique.

In the case of Bleach Bright, and again hypothetically, let's assume that various ads were developed around each story as directed by the three concepts above.

Without getting into the methodology, following a battery of questions, we would be interested especially in three areas of investigation: (1) The respondents' indication of their *intent to purchase* the brand the way it is advertised; (2) the respondents' evaluation of *how unique* or different the brand is as advertised; (3) the respondents' evaluation of how well they identify with the brand. This is usually discovered through answers to a question like *Is this brand for people like me?*

In general, *intent to purchase* is not always a good predictor of purchase behavior, since what we intend is not always what we do. But as a relative measure it can be very helpful, especially when differences between responses associated with each concept are dramatically different. In the case of Bleach Bright, let's assume that scores for *intent to purchase* for the brand as the Wizard archetype were found to be dramatically lower than for the other two concepts. Further investigating why, we might see that scores for uniqueness were also much lower than for the other two concepts, as respondents told us that what is described in the Wizard ads is something they've seen or heard before. We would then eliminate the Wizard idea from consideration.

Let's further assume that the tiebreaker between the remaining two concepts was found in answers to the *brand for people like me* question. Let's say that the brand as Emperor ads came out far ahead. Granted, the Emperor story would be sold to the smallest audience relative to the other two scenarios, but it is the concept that respondents best identify with and, as such, makes this story more appealing. The quantity of opportunity may be smaller, but the quality of opportunity is far bigger and presents fewer risks for the Emperor story, as configured in the circles.

Again, this example is oversimplified for the purposes of illustration. But it's meant to provide you with some sense of how to go about connecting the characters that you've considered in Step 2. Your analysis of both the quantity and quality of opportunity assesses both the chances of success and the chances of failure. Sometimes, the big opportunity can blind marketers to the latter.

As we've discussed, brands that are not aware of their limitations can make huge mistakes if they morph into something outside the realm of realistic possibilities. Step 3 forces one to systematically consider different strategic alternatives evaluating both risk and reward.

Review

- The brand and prospect cells have to be matched to achieve optimal results.

- A salad bar dilemma occurs when considering all the different combinations and permutations of brand and prospect matches.

- The challenge is to walk away with the best complements to each other, while avoiding a mixture of green peas with pineapples.

- Every brand story presents some risks.

- The purpose of Step 4, Connecting the Characters, is to identify opportunities while eliminating as much risk as possible.

- To do this, in Step 4, we assess both the quantity and the quality of the story's opportunity.

- The quantity assessment measures the size of the opportunity. The quality assessment measures the ease of persuasion.

STEP 5: CONFRONTING THE OBSTACLES

CHAPTER 14

The Obstacles

If you can find a path with no obstacles, it probably doesn't lead anywhere.
—Frank A. Clark

The hero's path is sometimes treacherous. Happy endings are the stuff of stories where someone defeats the fiery dragon, human malevolence, the dangers of nature, or technology gone wrong. But sometimes obstacles are more psychological than physical. Stories can also show how the hero's fear, greed, denial, or other negative human dispositions can stand in the way of success.

Brands, too, must deal with obstacles both physical and psychological on their way to achieve the goal of affiliation with the prospect. We also refer to this movement to overcome these obstacles as the brand's story plot. Whereas we've discussed the composition of the characters, in order to construct the plot, now we must survey the given obstacles. Marketing classicists divide these obstacles into two camps. First are the external obstacles, or those being exerted on the brand from outside forces such as competition, culture, the economy, or consumer attitudes and perceptions. Then are the internal obstacles that include things that are happening within the company that stand in the way of progress. These are usually a function of problems associated with production, distribution, and how the brand is marketed relative to the competition.

StoryBranding does not obviate the need to consider the classic barriers that most marketers will naturally consider. We did this when we described the backstory discussed in Chapter 7. But to remain true to story structure, StoryBranding reveals obstacles in a unique light, one that is related to the brand's primary goal of creating a strong and enduring relationship with the prospect.

Obstacles have levels, too.

We spoke of the staging of various connection milestones during the brand's product life cycle. The relationship connection between the prospect and the brand is made stronger as the prospect gains awareness of the product's function en route to an identification with the brand's belief system. To gain the desirable connection strength, we look at the individual obstacles that block or impede the brand–prospect relationship at each milestone.

THE FOUR OBSTACLES

The Level I Obstacle: No Product Function Awareness

With regard to the product function connection, the first obstacle encountered is the low-level awareness that exists for a new product that defines a new category. I provided a fictional account of the journey a man's wallet made on its way to Level IV. But we see this in real-life examples all the time. This is especially prevalent in the direct response commercials we see for new inventions like the ShamWow, the Snuggie, or the Ped Egg. There's never been anything quite like these products before, so creating awareness of their primary function is the single most important feat that must be accomplished.

The Level II Obstacle: No Product Superiority Comprehension

At the next level, the product superiority connection, the obstacle is a lack of comprehension about why the brand's product is perhaps better than competitive offerings. In classic marketing-speak, this is often referred to as getting the prospect to understand the brand's unique selling proposition vis-à-vis competition. This usually takes place as the product moves from the introductory or growth stage of its life cycle.

The Level III Obstacle: Lack of Brand Association

Level III is where brand considerations first come into play. Often referred to as the confidence obstacle, what is often standing in the way between the brand and the prospect is a lack of positive association with the brand itself. This could result from any number of causes, from something as simple as a lack of familiarity with the brand name to something as complex as outright disbelief.

At times, the brand deals with Level II and Level III obstacles simultaneously. Level II obstacles occur when the product advantage is presented with a cogent argument and no preexisting conditions impede the brand. Level III obstacles arise from either direct or indirect experiences with the brand. We will avoid some brands regardless of their superiority claims, simply because we've had bad experiences with them in the past or have heard negative stories about them from others.

One can readily discern the extent to which Level III obstacles are in the way by interviewing prospects to determine what word associations exist for the brand name. It's one thing to measure meaning associations, but it's also very important to measure the strength of those associations. You might find, for instance, that your brand is positively associated with words like "status," "sexy," or "superior." But take it one step further. Find out how strong those associations are by gauging how certain prospects feel about these associations. There's a huge difference between someone who thinks of your brand as superior and someone who firmly believes it to be true. Do the same for negative associations as well.

The Level IV Obstacle: Lack of Brand Affiliation

A failure to achieve the final connection, the prized Level IV affiliation, is usually due to the marketer's simply having ignored its importance. Many brands get stuck at Level III because they think it's the finish line. "If we can only get the prospect to see that we truly are superior, we'll win market share," goes the thinking. So R&D struggles to come up with a new and improved formula, operations develops a better way to service the customer, or distribution figures out a way to get more facings in the supermarket.

Certainly, ongoing innovation is important. If any traction is gained in Level III, it is short-lived. The differentiating benefit that knocked down that Level III obstacle today will sooner or later be copied by a competitor tomorrow or become obsolete in and of itself. Dealing with Level III obstacles is like a game of Whack-a-Mole. Knock one down and another comes up.

A tactic often employed when all else fails to overcome the Level III obstacle is reducing the price. This is like throwing up the white flag of surrender and an indication that the brand hasn't been able to get beyond a Level III connection. Besides sacrificing margins, too much reliance on price reductions can have a deleterious effect on the brand. It's better to find ways to propel the brand into a Level IV connection than to remain stuck in Level III.

For those more enlightened brands that see the Level IV connection as something worth pursuing, failure rears its head simply because the brand is trying to associate with values and beliefs that can't be substantiated through their outer layers, as discussed in chapter 11. This is the authenticity problem we discussed earlier. Other brands seeing Level IV as the goal line find it elusive because they are trying too hard to attain it. To be achieved, identification has to be felt by the prospect. Resonance can't be forced. Attempts to do so will be resisted and can push the brand all the way back to Level II. McDonald's was smart to abandon its "We love to make you smile" campaign before it did too much damage. For many it was hyperbolic nonsense, given the operational problems that McDonald's was facing at the time.

To get through obstacles to making a strong Level IV connection, the belief that the brand stands for must link to a belief that the prospect considers to be personally important. It must represent an important human value the prospect readily identifies with. Additionally, it must be uniquely believable and authentically communicated through the brand's behavior or its outer layer. Once at Level IV, the brand will achieve a long-term proprietary association that is impossible for competitors to copy without looking like an also-ran.

SUCCESS BEGETS SUCCESS

Although I've presented these obstacles in sequential order, they all must be dealt with simultaneously. In the beginning, when a brand sets out to make a functional product connection, be mindful that other obstacles will show up right around the corner. I am not suggesting that brands ought to knock down all four obstacles at the same time. Brands that try to do this try to do too much at once. However, unless all possible obstacles are considered up front, the brand will be unprepared to deal with the oncoming storm. In the worst case, the brand will be defined in terms of its product features and benefits alone. This will make it difficult to branch out with other products with the same brand name.

This is what happened to Polaroid, as it became known solely for its ability to provide instant still pictures. When it introduced a video camera, it couldn't get past the confidence obstacle because it wasn't seen as a brand that could effectively compete in the video space. Prospects questioned its ability to provide a good video camera because their association with Polaroid was relegated solely to still cameras. Xerox, a name synonymous with copier machines, ran into the same problem when it tried to introduce computers.

Apple, on the other hand, has always stood for the value of "thinking different." Consequently, this worked well in the beginning when Apple was competing with the likes of IBM and during the introduction of its Macintosh computer. But this value is also what continues to help Apple hurdle the obstacles it faces each time it introduces a new product. Now, for instance, when Apple introduces a product like its iPhone or iPad, prospects knock down the obstacles themselves. Any product branded with the Apple name quickly gets through the first three obstacles on the way to a Level IV connection.

Apple didn't run into the same problem that Xerox ran into because from the beginning Apple stood for something much bigger than just one product. It stood for a belief that embraces everything it offers. Apple exemplifies the value of thinking ahead and envisioning where it ultimately wants to go. By deciding what it stood for, the Apple brand effectively paved the way for itself to bigger fortunes and to Level IV connections with its prospects. For the Apple loyalist customer, Apple could probably introduce an edible athletic shoe that would get instant acceptance.

Review

- StoryBranding reveals obstacles in a unique light, one that is related to the brand's primary goal of creating a strong and enduring relationship with the prospect.

- With regard to the product function connection, the first obstacle encountered is the low-level awareness that exists for a new product that defines a new category.

- At the product superiority connection level, the obstacle is a lack of comprehension about why the brand's product is perhaps better than competitive offerings.

- A Level III connection occurs when positive and meaningful associations are attributed to the brand.

- To achieve brand affiliation, the Level IV connection, identification has to be felt by the prospect. Resonance can't be forced. Attempts to do so will be resisted and can push the brand all the way back to Level II.

- To get through obstacles to make a strong Level IV connection, the belief that the brand stands for must link to a belief that the prospect also considers important.

- In the beginning, when a brand sets out to make a functional product connection, be mindful that other obstacles will show up right around the corner.

STEP 6: COMPLETING THE STORYBRIEF

CHAPTER 15

The StoryBrief

The outline is 95 percent of the book. Then I sit down
and write, and that's the easy part.
—Jeffery Deaver, American mystery and crime writer

By now you are ready to execute the StoryBrief. The StoryBrief, similar to the traditional creative brief, provides a summary of strategic thought and sets up the expectations for the brand's messaging. But that's the only thing they have in common. The StoryBrief is significantly different.

As a summary of all the preceding steps in the StoryBranding process, it defines the elements of the brand's story. As such, it identifies both the brand's and prospect's inner and outer layers. Additionally, it defines the most important communication obstacles that have to be confronted for the brand to move closer to achieving a strong and enduring relationship with the prospect.

Some have argued that the typical, traditional creative brief's purpose is very similar in that it asks for an identification of the prospect, how he or she thinks and feels, and what the brand has to claim in order to reinforce, change, or create its appeal. However, the difference is twofold.

First, the StoryBrief is constructed very differently as it identifies the story cells that have been analyzed and defined and together will create the brand's story.

Second is the difference in how the questions are asked and answered. As you can see from the graphic depiction of the StoryBrief on the following pages, there are 6 very different questions that need to be answered. These all lead up to the definition of the Unique Value Proposition (UVP), or the central idea behind the brand's story.

As you read through this graphic, you'll notice that questions 3 and 6 ask for written "I AM statements," one for the brand character and the other for the prospect respectively. Both I AM statements are written in the first person. The reason for this will become apparent to you as you become more familiar with I AM statements, but suffice it to say, the intent is to facilitate empathy. In this way, our understanding of the brand and the brand's prospect goes well beyond factual explanations that are the subject of traditional briefs. As such, the I AM statements are critical components of the StoryBrief and are discussed separately in the next two chapters.

The Unique Value Proposition is shown in this graphic as the end result of the 6 preceding questions. The UVP is a simple sentence or phrase that defines the value or belief with which the brand is to be associated. Whereas it is a "simple" sentence, writing it is the most challenging task in the StoryBranding process.

If you followed the StoryBranding Process up to this point, the StoryBrief should be nothing more than a summarization exercise. In short-sentence form, it asks you to state what you've learned and decisions you've already made about everything except the UVP. The UVP has yet to be discussed. To help you better grapple with your brand's UVP, make certain to read Chapter 18. In addition to reading about the UVP in depth, I've provided some helpful thought triggers.

What follows is a more detailed description of the six questions than shown in the graphic, with two examples before I AM Statements are written. The I AM examples for each are shown in Chapter 17.

If you'd like to download Page 1 of this StoryBrief graphic for easy reference, you can download it from my blog at www.storyati.com.

The StoryBrief

1. The Backstory: What is the brand's current situation and how did it get there? What do we know about the prospect today? (Review chapter 6 for all pertinent information to be discussed.)

_____

2. Define the brand's inner layer: What value or important belief does the brand champion? If you used archetypal analysis, state the archetypal definition of the brand. Provide rationale.

_____

3. Define the brand's outer layer: How is the inner layer supported by the product's (or the products') advantages and benefits? Explain why the outer layer is congruent with the inner layer. Write the Brand I AM statement.

_____

4. What are the most important obstacles? Given the overall objective of establishing a strong relationship with the prospect, to what extent are the following obstacles still standing in the way? Explain your answers and use this scale to evaluate: 1 = very low and 5 = very high.
   a. Product Function Awareness: To what extent does the prospect know what the product's function is?

   _____

   b. Product Benefit Comprehension: To what extent does the prospect know what the product's unique functional benefits are?

   _____

THE STORYBRIEF

1. THE BACKSTORY

How did the brand get to where it is today and what are its goals for the future? Include all background information on competition and category trends.

ASSEMBLING IDEAS

2. DEFINING THE BRAND'S INNER LAYER

What value or important belief does the brand champion? If you use archetypal analysis, state the archetypal definition of the brand. Provide rationale.

6. DEFINE THE PROSPECT'S INNER LAYER

■ Define the prospect's most important functional need.
■ Make certain this need is consistent with the brand's inner layer.

Define Unique Value Proposition

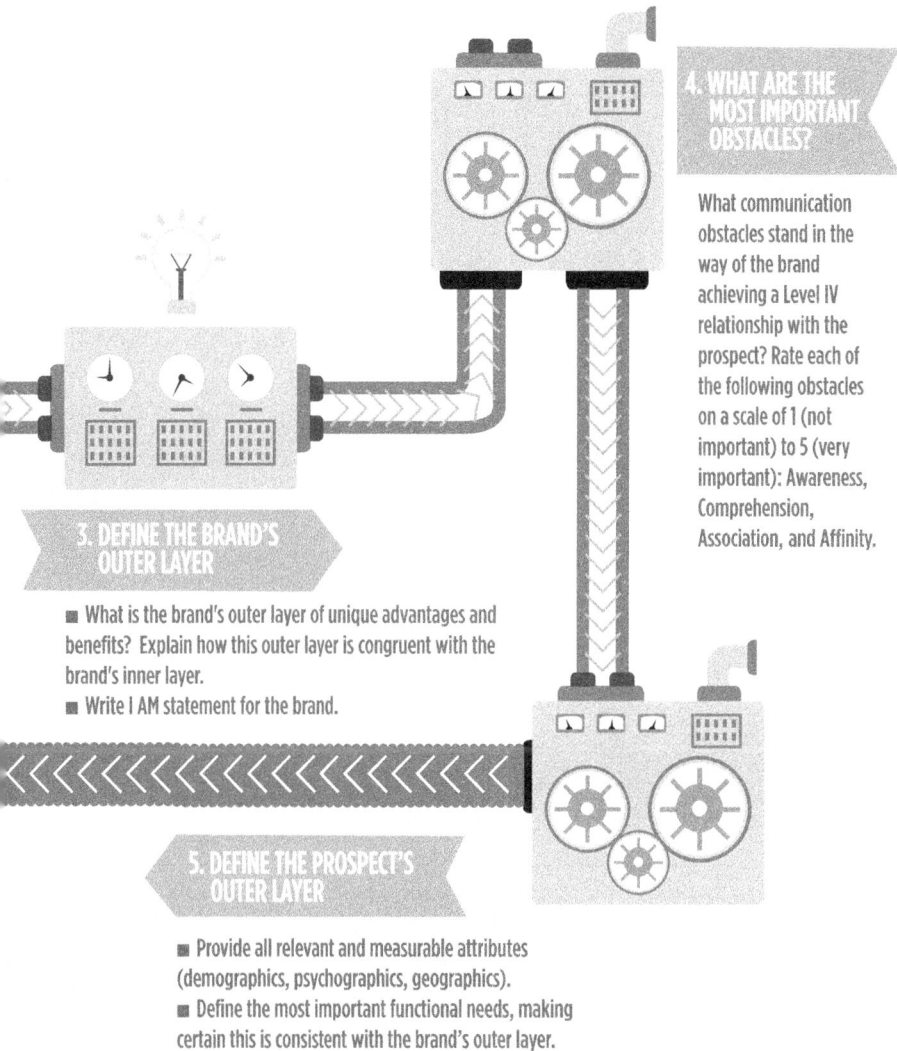

4. WHAT ARE THE MOST IMPORTANT OBSTACLES?

What communication obstacles stand in the way of the brand achieving a Level IV relationship with the prospect? Rate each of the following obstacles on a scale of 1 (not important) to 5 (very important): Awareness, Comprehension, Association, and Affinity.

3. DEFINE THE BRAND'S OUTER LAYER

■ What is the brand's outer layer of unique advantages and benefits? Explain how this outer layer is congruent with the brand's inner layer.
■ Write I AM statement for the brand.

5. DEFINE THE PROSPECT'S OUTER LAYER

■ Provide all relevant and measurable attributes (demographics, psychographics, geographics).
■ Define the most important functional needs, making certain this is consistent with the brand's outer layer.

    c. Brand Association: What are the current associations with the brand, and how strong are these associations?

_____

    d. Brand Affiliation: To what extent does the prospect have a deep relationship with the brand?

_____

    e. Understanding that brand affiliation is the long-term goal, considering your answers from *a* through *c*, what is the most important obstacle(s) that must also be overcome in the short-term?

_____

5. Define the prospect's outer layer:

    a. Provide all relevant and measurable attributes (e.g., age range, sex, income, family size, income, geography, etc.).

_____

    b. What is the most important function that the prospect would want to achieve with the brand's product (or products)? Make certain that this is consistent with the brand's outer layer.

_____

6. Define the prospect's inner layer: What is the most important and relevant value/belief that the prospect subscribes to? Make certain this is consistent with the brand's inner layer. Write the Prospect I AM statement.

_____

EXAMPLE 1

Here is an example of a StoryBrief for Bleach Bright, the fictitious brand of laundry detergent discussed in the previous chapter:

StoryBrief for Bleach Bright

1. The Backstory: What is the brand's current situation and how
    did it get there? What do we know about the prospect today?
    (Review chapter 6 for all pertinent information to be discussed.)

    *Bleach Bright is a new brand of laundry detergent manufactured by
    Practical Gamble. It will compete in a category that has many well-entrenched
    competitors (e.g., Tibe and Bliz), which are also manufactured by Practical
    Gamble and lead market share with 32 percent and 24 percent, respectively.*

    *Studies have shown that color brightness is the most desirable
    attribute when it comes to laundry detergent, especially among working
    women. From studies conducted within this segment, brightness is
    associated with feeling confident.*

    *Currently many brands are claiming that they make clothes cleaner
    and brighter (see competitive ads attached). Practical Gamble believes
    that Bleach Bright, with its unique bleach crystals, albeit cannibalistic
    to its existing brands, can steal share from other laundry detergent
    manufacturers. Many laundry detergents get clothes clean. But they do
    this while dulling whites and colors over time. Bleach Bright's unique
    bleach crystals have been tested to show that both colors and whites
    come out brighter than with other detergents, wash after wash. In a test
    of twenty washes, Bleach Bright clothes came out 15 percent brighter
    than those using the leading laundry detergent with bleach (measured in
    lumens). The reason for this is that Bleach Bright crystals are formulated
    to work harder on whites and colors than other bleach products do.*

    *The brand will be introduced in three test markets (to be
    determined) with the same campaign.*

    *Practical Gamble spends a great deal on research and development
    and puts a lot of weight on proven performance before introducing new
    products. Management, being highly formalized, believes that new
    products must pass a number of internal financial, operational, and
    performance tests before going to market.*

2. Define the brand's inner layer: What value or important belief does the brand champion? If you used archetypal analysis, state the archetypal definition of the brand. Provide rationale.

   Bleach Bright will be associated with the Emperor archetype. It champions the values of confidence and accomplishment. The belief can be summed up as "looking good feels good, and feeling good about oneself is empowering."

3. Define the brand's outer layer: How is the inner layer supported by the product's (or the products') advantages and benefits? Explain why the outer layer is congruent with the inner layer.

   Brighter clothes enhance confidence. Tests have shown that Bleach Bright delivers 15 percent more brightness than the next brightest detergent does.

   The brand I AM statement is shown in Chapter 17.

4. What are the most important obstacles? Given the overall objective of establishing a strong affinitive relationship with the prospect, to what extent are the following obstacles still standing in the way? Explain your answers and use this scale to evaluate: 1 = very low and 5 = very high.

   a. Product Function Awareness: To what extent does the prospect know what the product's function is?

      Rating: 5—Everyone knows what laundry detergent is for.

   b. Product Benefit Comprehension: To what extent does the prospect know what the product's unique functional benefits are?

      Rating: 1—Bleach Bright is a new product and has no consumer awareness or benefit comprehension, as yet. Specifically, there is very low comprehension of bleach crystals and their advantages.

c. Brand Associations: What are the current associations with the brand, and how strong are these associations?

Prospects currently associate Bleach Bright with words like "clean," "white," and "bright." But those associations are very weak and are more a function of the brand name than any real experience with the brand.

Rating: 2—Because nobody is aware of the brand as yet, confidence in the brand is nonexistent. However, consumers have very high confidence in Practical Gamble as a manufacturer that could rub off on the brand.

d. Brand Affiliation: To what extent does the product have a strong relationship with the brand?

Rating: 1—Because the brand is nonexistent, brand affiliation has not yet been established.

e. Understanding that brand affiliation is the long-term goal, and considering your answers from *a* through *c*, what is the most important obstacle(s) that must also be overcome in the short-term?

Product Benefit Comprehension. Prospect should become aware of the advantages and benefits of Bleach Bright's unique bleach crystals.

5. Define the prospect's outer layer:

a. Provide all relevant and measurable attributes (e.g., age range, sex, income, family size, income, geography, etc.). Write the prospect I AM statement.

Female, 25–49, single or married, professional, living in A and B counties throughout the United States.

b. What is the most important function that the prospect would want to achieve with the brand's product (or products)? Make certain this is consistent with the brand's outer layer.

Brighter clothes.

The prospect I AM statement is shown in Chapter 17.

6. Define the prospect's inner layer: What is the most important and relevant value/belief that the prospect subscribes to? Make certain this is consistent with the brand's inner layer.

That looking good is important to the success of a working woman. The second example is in stark contrast to the Bleach Bright example. Here, instead of a business-to-consumer brand, we have a business-to-business brand. Furthermore, we have a brand that is fairly well entrenched vs. one that is new. And we have an established product that is underperforming.

EXAMPLE 2

StoryBrief for The Maverick by National Trucks

1. The Backstory: What is the brand's current situation and how did it get there? What do we know about the prospect today?

National Truck is regarded as the leading heavy-duty, long-haul truck manufacturer as measured in sales and leases to transportation companies. National's trucks are believed to have the lowest cost of operation (LCO) and the most liberal maintenance warranty of all trucks on the market.

Two years ago, National Truck decided to market a truck dedicated to the independent owner-operator. Owner-operators are highly self-reliant, rugged individualist types. They believe that working for a trucking company is a sellout.

At the time the Maverick was introduced, owner-operators regarded National Trucks as "the 18-wheel vanilla," meaning they were stripped of the functional and aesthetic appeal that owner-operators typically look for in a truck. To the owner-operator segment, National Trucks were "too corporate."

To counter this perception, the Maverick was introduced as their black sheep truck and was positioned as the Bad Boy (see competitive ads). Unlike the typical National truck, the Maverick was black on black. It also came with a unique flame-decaled exterior and chrome mud flaps. It had leather seats that reclined into a queen-size bed with mattress vibrator, a sixteen-speaker stereo system, a DVD player, and a small refrigerator. Except for the mattress vibrator, trucks normally sold to the owner-operator also had many of the same features, however.

Sales are currently well below projections. Surveys show that the truck competes well in price and features with the truck brands that the owner-operator is used to buying; however, the fact that it is manufactured by National poses the biggest problem.

Also, at this time, gas prices have skyrocketed and have eaten into owner-operator profits. This fact alone has resulted in a 15 percent decline in the number of owner-operators. Many, in order to survive, have had to start working for the corporate transportation companies that they've long despised. The Maverick can show that, on average, it can save a trucker $10,000 a year in operating expenses.

2. Define the brand's inner layer: What value or important belief does the brand champion? If you used archetypal analysis, state the archetypal definition of the brand. Provide rationale.

   Independence and Comfort. The Rebel (Explorer)—the Maverick keeps independent truckers from having to be fenced in working for somebody else, while allowing them the comforts they've become used to.

3. Define the brand's outer layer: How is the inner layer supported by the product's (or the products') advantages and benefits? Explain why the outer layer is congruent with the inner layer.

    The Maverick is a high-performing truck, with all the comforts that the owner-operator wants, but with the LCO that owner-operators need.

4. What are the most important obstacles? Given the overall objective of establishing a strong affinitive relationship with the prospect, to what extent are the following obstacles standing in the way? Explain your answers and use this scale to evaluate: 1 = very low and 5 = very high.

    a. Product Function Awareness: To what extent does the prospect know what the product's function is?
        Rating: 5

    b. Product Benefit Comprehension: To what extent does the prospect know what the product's unique functional benefits are?
        Rating: 4—National has a strong association with LCO among all truck drivers.

    c. Brand Associations: What are the current associations with the brand, and how strong are these associations?
        Rating: 5—It's a "National." Great for LCO, but the image of National comes with some negative baggage for the owner-operator. And that association is very strong.

d. Brand Affiliation: To what extent does the product have a strong relationship with the brand?

Rating: 1—Because it's made by National, it represents corporate values that many owner-operators are opposed to.

e. Understanding that brand affiliation is the long-term goal, and considering your answers from a through c, what is the most important obstacle(s) that must also be overcome in the short-term?

Brand association and affiliation.

5. Define the prospect's outer layer:

a. Provide all relevant and measurable attributes.

Owner-operators who have a neutral or better disposition toward National and who place a great deal of importance on LCO.

b. What is the most important function that the prospect would want to achieve with the brand's product (or products)? Make certain this is consistent with the brand's outer layer.

LCO in a truck made for owner-operators.

6. Define the prospect's inner layer: What is the most important and relevant value/belief that the prospect subscribes to? Make certain this is consistent with the brand's inner layer.

This is the segment of independent, self-reliant owner-operators who, out of necessity, have come to realize the importance of fuel efficiency. Their belief is that price should not get in the way of good business sense.

Let's turn to the I AM statements.

Review

- As a a summary of all the preceding steps in the StoryBranding Process, the StoryBrief defines the elements of the brand's story.

- Additionally, it defines the most important communication obstacles that have to be confronted by the brand to move it closer to achieving a strong and enduring relationship with the prospect.

- The StoryBrief consists of six questions that must be answered before defining the Unique Selling Proposition (UVP).

- If you've followed the StoryBranding Process up to this point, completing the StoryBrief should be nothing more than a summarization process.

CHAPTER 16

I AM Statements

The great gift of human beings is that we have the power of empathy.
—Meryl Streep

Meryl Streep should know a lot about the subject of empathy. She's made it her profession. And having been nominated for more Academy Awards and Golden Globes than any other actor (sixteen and twenty-five, respectively, as of this writing), I'd say she's pretty good at what she does.

Whereas Streep was undoubtedly born with a prodigious talent, she didn't just fall out of bed one day to become one of the modern era's greatest empathizers. She traveled a long road—studying, training, and transforming her gift into a powerful skill. And along the way, she picked up a number of techniques or acting methods that help her identify with her characters in a way that allows her to embrace them.

I'm not an expert on acting—I'm just a fan. But from watching (and rewatching) countless films over a lifetime, it seems to me that there are at least two important steps for creating a character: observation and immersion.

Observation is what Dustin Hoffman did for months as he learned about savants for his role in *Rain Man*. To prepare, he met with Kim Peek, the man his character was based on, and studied numerous narratives and documentaries on savants. But observations have to be translated into actions. And that's where immersion comes in. To become his character, Hoffman didn't just *see and do*. He went through an extensive process that involved creating specific physical gestures, experimenting with hair and wardrobe, developing a unique vocal quality, thinking about motivations and emotional responses, and probably hundreds of other things that made his performance so magical. And then, of course, he spent endless hours internalizing and practicing all of this. Ultimately, through immersion, he achieved empathy. And the line between him and the character he portrayed disappeared.

Any number of observational techniques are available to us—focus groups, surveys, specialized research methods like thematic apperception, anthropological approaches, etc. They all have their merits. But they are not enough. To achieve a higher degree of empathy, we also need immersion.

For marketers, immersion is often limited to buying or using their own and competitor's products. Certainly this is helpful in understanding the user experience. But we can still do more to stimulate what scientists have recently described as our brain's mirror neurons. Mirror neurons explain why we might sit on the edge of our seats during a suspense thriller, or why those of us who can admit it get choked up during certain scenes. They are also stimulated when someone describes an experience in such a way that we can feel what they felt. This is where I AM statements are particularly valuable.

From your first experience writing I AM statements, you will quickly discover that they are more than mere writing exercises. Writing I AM statements provides a valuable immersion experience as you think and feel like the character you are describing. While writing them, I AM statements allow us to try on the individual psyches of the brand story's characters to see how they fit. And because they are written as first-person narratives, they force us to identify with the characters in ways that simple explanations cannot.

If you read chapter 1, you were briefly introduced to an example of a prospect I AM statement in the case of the Last National Bank. It is responsible for paving the way to what is now the StoryBranding process. Writing I AM statements is one of the most important tasks asked for by this process. In addition to writing an I AM statement for the prospect, we also write one for the brand character.

For the brand, writing an I AM statement helps us to relate to the brand as a person. No matter how the brand is described, as long as it is described in the third person, a brand remains a thing. Writing about the brand as a person imbues it with beliefs and values that humans possess. I've rarely seen a traditional creative brief that has captured the full and unique essence of the brand's character. More often than not, I'll see something like "XYZ Fast Food Company brand position: XYZ is the brand of fast food that provides real, wholesome, delicious food that our customers crave," or "ABC Car brand position: The ABC is 'first in class' as it defines what luxury and performance are all about."

Keep in mind that the goal of the brand's story is to achieve a Level IV connection, one that forms a lasting relationship with the prospect. It is hard to see how this can happen when brands are poorly defined in a creative brief. People do not form relationships with fast food restaurants, cars, or any branded object's positioning. Rather, they form relationships with what the brand means to them in human terms.

If you have navigated the StoryBranding process, you have already outlined the content for the two I AM statements that have to be written. The information they will contain is found in the inner and outer layers of each character's cells. The I AM statement organizes and translates this information into language that your brand story's characters would use to describe both what they do and why they do it.

HOW TO WRITE I AM STATEMENTS

I'm going to offer a number of suggestions on how to write I AM statements. But the most important among these is to just go with it. I once heard a famous novelist who was being interviewed say that his characters write themselves. *That sounds so poetic, so prophetic, so something-an-author-might-say to sound like their talents are channeled*, I thought. But, lo and behold, while writing I AM statements, I continue to find this phenomenon to be true. Typically, I will start out with some idea of where I'm going, but more often than not, as I try to think and feel like the character, I find myself going off into places I couldn't possibly imagine from the start. So, my advice is to let the I AM statement take you where you need to go. And may the Force be with you.

I realize that letting go is easier for some than others. Nevertheless, it's an important challenge to meet head-on. With practice, it comes quite naturally. For starters, I always recommend writing an I AM statement for yourself. Besides helping you define your personal brand, your own I AM statement can serve as training wheels and will help you to better understand the process. Consider some audience that you want to impress with who you are and what you stand for, maybe a prospective employer or your boss. Start with the words I AM and have at it. Your resume of accomplishments provides much of the content for your outer layer. And the beliefs and values that those accomplishments manifest make up your inner layer.

Another exercise that helps is to take a word that represents a belief or value, such as *independence* or *caring*, and write as if you were those values. Start with "I AM independence" and free-flow your ideas on what being independence feels like.

WRITING THE PROSPECT AND BRAND I AM STATEMENTS

When you're ready, you needn't be too concerned about which of the two necessary I AM statements to start with. I do favor a certain order. But however you approach writing I AM statements, the most important thing to keep in mind is that the prospect's and the brand's statements should complement each other. Once completed, the two I AM statements that you've written should provide proof that such a strong relationship has every reason to exist.

To ensure that the prospect's and brand's outer layers are consistent with each other, I usually start by writing about both of the outer layers first. Then, I move on to write about the inner layers. To help you organize the data that you've already gathered, you can use the following steps as a guideline:

THE PROSPECT'S OUTER LAYER

1. Start with the demographics, for example, "I AM between the ages of twenty-five and thirty-four, and I am male or female, married with two kids, and my income is more than $75,000." If you're familiar with what is often referred to as a persona, I AM statements are different. In a persona, you write about one person who might be within your target. I AM statements aggregate all of your prospects to provide a more generalized picture of the mass audience represented by what you've defined as the brand's prospect. I AM statements, for reasons already discussed are also written in the first-person.

2. Speaking as the prospect, you have a functional problem that needs to be solved. Explain what the problem is and why a solution is needed. Get into the problem, and experience it as your prospect would. Try to think and feel as he or she does. For example: *Having my computer go down is unacceptable. When it goes down, I'm out of business, let alone out of touch with my world. The last thing I need is someone to tell me that they'll get back to me in a week with an estimate. I need it now!*

    Err on the side of too much information. You can make it more succinct later.

3. What does successfully accomplishing the character's goal look like? How does that make you feel? Express this in an *I wish* statement. Exaggerate, if necessary, for example: *I wish I could just hit some button from inside my house to start my car on cold days.*

4. What is your character's experience with the product if it is being used currently or has been used in the past? For example: *I found the food at the Hamburger Joint to be no better than any other place that claims they make "gourmet" hamburgers.*

5. Is your character aware of your and/or competitors' brands? If so, what do you know about how it is perceived relative to competitive offerings? For example: *I think Apple computers are easier to use than PCs.*

6. Are there any thoughts your character has about your brand that are erroneous? For example: *The Mini Cooper is small. It must not be very fast.*

7. Are there any feelings that your character has about your product, or products like yours? For example: *I love my Keurig coffee machine because I don't have to wait a long time for the coffee to be made.*

THE BRAND'S OUTER LAYER

1. Start by defining what the product is by talking about features that are consistent with the prospect's needs. For example: *I am a speedy oil change for people in a hurry.*

2. Provide the rational support points for why this product can solve the prospect's stated problem. For example: *I'm the simple, well-illustrated manual for people who need fast help with their computers.*

3. Speaking as the brand, explain what success will look like for the prospect. For example: *I'm what people need to have the white teeth that make them more attractive.*

4. Talk about the advantages that you have over competitive alternatives. For example: *I'm the easiest and fastest way to get your car waxed and shined.*

5. If applicable, talk about experiences current customers have had with your product. For example: *I have been ranked highest by J.D. Powers for customer satisfaction three years in a row.*

6. Provide information that counters any misperceptions about the product that the prospect might have. For example: *I'm not a gas guzzler. I get 25 miles per gallon.*

This is what we call the *brag and boast* portion of the brand's I AM statement. It is pure, unadulterated selling as we've always known it. Brag away and edit later.

From here, though, I then start writing about the inner layers. I find it easiest to start with the brand first, but often go back and forth between the brand's inner layer description and the prospect's inner layer description to ensure consistency. The writing becomes a little more challenging while navigating the inner layers of both characters. The reason for this is that you will no longer be dealing in the realm of the tangible, provable, or rational. Things get more abstract when you start to write about beliefs and values. But that essentially is what is required. Here again are some guidelines for how to describe the inner layers.

THE PROSPECT'S INNER LAYER

1. Talk about the values you subscribe to that are consistent with the brand's beliefs about what is important. Explain why these values are regarded as important. For example: *I am ethical and law-abiding and care about the environment.*

2. Make certain what you've written as your prospect's outer layer serves as proof of what you stand for. The problem you are trying to solve should be reflected in your inner layer. For example: *I worry about my family's welfare.*

3. The most important ingredient of the inner layer is empathy. Immerse yourself in what it must be like to be this person. Ladder up from what you said in the outer layer to why it is important. Explain what you mean. Don't just say, "I believe it's important to look and feel my best." Explain why. Say something such as, *I know that it's just human nature for people to make judgments about who I am based on the way I look. They'll never know my book by its cover, but at least they'll see they're in the right section of the library.*

4. Draw on metaphors or comparisons to real things to make the intangible more concrete. For example: *I'm one of a kind in a good way. I like to think of myself as a diamond in the rough.*

THE BRAND'S INNER LAYER

Take from the archetypal description of your brand all information that explains what it is that you, as your brand, stand for and believe in. Go back to the archetypes and use the *sayings they might live by* as a springboard. You can even use those sayings verbatim if you like.

To get further inspired, I pick out a word that represents a value, say, *accomplishment*, and search the Internet for quotes, ideas, and/or thoughts about what accomplishment is all about.

Make certain that what you've written as your brand's outer layer serves as the proof of what you stand for. Remember, the reason the outer layer exists is because of the inner layer. It is critical that outer and inner layers be congruent.

VOICE

The primary idea behind writing I AM statements is to become the prospect and the brand. Try to write like they would talk. Don't get prosaic if your character is a plumber.

Use conversational slang, jargon, even bad grammar if and when appropriate. Pretend you're talking instead of writing, if it helps. Go for sound, rhythm, and pace. Read it out loud a few times. Ask someone to listen to you to see if it sounds authentic. This may seem overdone at first. But how the I AM statement reads is as important as what it says. In truth, how it sounds is a very important part of what it says.

THE EDITING PROCESS

Once you've written the I AM statements, it is important to realize that these will become something that other people associated with the brand will eventually work with. Before you hand out a twelve-page, double-spaced paper on the subject, think about all of those instruction manuals that you never read and why you didn't read them. If details are important, keep them succinct. Do not be redundant. And, by all means, use paragraphs to separate thoughts.

Review

- Writing I AM statements provides a valuable immersion experience as you think and feel like the character you are describing.

- People do not form relationships with fast-food restaurants, cars, or any branded object's positioning. Rather, they form relationships with what the brand means to them in human terms.

- However you approach writing I AM statements, the most important thing to keep in mind is that the prospect's and the brand's statements should complement each other.

- Get into the prospect's problem; experience it as your prospect would. Try to think and feel as he or she does.

- The brand's outer layer is what we call the *brag and boast* portion of the brand's I AM statement. It is pure, unadulterated selling as we've always known it. Brag away and edit later.

- If details are important, keep them succinct. The purpose of the I AM statement is to evoke empathy. Try to write the way the prospect would talk.

CHAPTER 17

I AM Examples

In this chapter, I've provided examples of I AM statements written by members of our staff. To protect the interests of our clients, we couldn't provide live examples, so we opted to create I AM statements for both the fictitious Bleach Bright and Maverick brands for which StoryBriefs were shown earlier. Keep in mind that these are written from assumption and conjecture. They are provided merely to offer some additional guidance.

Clearly, writing I AM statements is an art form. However, this is an exercise you will become more adept at as you practice. If your experience is anything like mine, you'll know when you nail them. Note how these I AM statements are highly consistent, with definitions provided in their respective StoryBriefs. At the same time, they provide the necessary color to enhance empathy and understanding.

I AM THE BLEACH BRIGHT PROSPECT

Life is hectic. Balancing my day-to-day responsibilities at home and at work leaves little time for anything else. When it comes to balancing life's mundane chores—whether it's dishes, dusting, or laundry—I want to spend as little time as possible getting them done. But like everything else I do, they have to be done right.

I require products that live up to their promises. That's why I tend to buy from companies I trust. I am willing to try new things, but I must be convinced that I'm not wasting my time or money. Whether it's the cheapest or most expensive doesn't matter. I just want the best.

Professionally, I have a vision of success. And I put a lot of energy into making it happen. When I give a presentation, close a sale, or make a promise of any kind, I want my customers to believe that I'll deliver 100 percent of the time.

What my customers see of me is as important as what I say. What I wear reflects who I am. And the person I must project is someone who is bright, confident, and capable.

When I reach into my closet, I need to know that my clothes are as perfect as the day I bought them: no tears, stains, or fading. I don't have time to fix my clothes. I don't have time to redo my laundry. I don't have time to waste. Period.

I'm fairly satisfied with the detergent I've been using, and I've rarely switched. Right now, I see no reason to. It satisfactorily performs the functions I need.

I AM BLEACH BRIGHT DETERGENT

You've never heard of me. More importantly, you've never heard of what I can do to improve the way your clothes look. Any number of detergents on the market can get clothes clean. But keeping colors bright is another matter. My unique bleach crystals have been tested to show that both colors and whites come out brighter than other detergents, wash after wash. In fact, in a test of twenty washes, clothes washed using me came out 15 percent brighter than with the leading laundry detergent with bleach. The reason for this is found in my unique crystals formulated to work harder on whites and colors than other bleach products. People who buy me are like me. I believe in the power of confidence, and so do they.

For my customers, "good enough" is never great, and they want great. For them, a lot depends on confidence. Portraying confidence says, "This is a person who is competent and can be trusted." The way a person looks won't instill confidence by itself, but looking the part goes a long way toward living the part. The self-assurance that comes from wearing clothes that are noticeably clean and bright versus dull and drabby is the most important reason I exist.

I AM THE PROSPECT FOR THE MAVERICK

When I became an operator of my own truck, it was like getting a new lease on life. No more bad routes. I could choose where I wanted to go, when, and what I wanted to haul. The days of toeing the corporate line were gone, and hopefully forever.

I got me a great rig, too. With all the comforts of home. Hell, some homes don't even have these comforts. No more vanilla trucks that say, "Hey, I'm just a corporate peon." I got me a truck that says, "I don't work for the man 'cause I AM the man!" But independence don't come easy. I'm running a business now. And a lot depends on it besides my pride.

I hear too many stories about guys like me having to go back to the corporate world because they can't make it. Especially now with gas prices being what they are.

There's them that say, "So what! The prices will come down 'cause they always do." But for me, losing my independence ain't worth the gamble. The last guy standing is the one who wins in this game. And if

I'm not going to be the last guy, I'm going to rank pretty close to it. Sure, I'd like to keep this cab. It's been like a member of my family. But better to be smart than broke. I'm going to stay in business for myself, no matter what it takes. And if it takes selling this rig for something that's going to help keep me in business, then I'll do it. I just hope I don't have to give up too much of what I've become used to.

I AM THE MAVERICK

There's no hiding the fact that I am made by National Trucks, the truck that is preferred by long-haul transportation companies. The reason for that is that my trucks consistently provide the lowest cost of operation. These days, with gas prices going up and more owner-operators going down, I don't make apologies for being who I am. In fact, I'm doing more to keep independent truckers from losing their independence than any truck on the road. Compare my numbers to anyone else's, and you'll see that I can save a trucker as much as $10,000 in operating expenses. Furthermore, while my efficiencies keep truckers truckin', I provide the same, if not better, creature comforts that can be found in trucks commonly preferred by the independent trucker. My all-black cabs come with leather seats that recline into a queen-size bed with a mattress vibrator, a sixteen-speaker stereo system, a DVD player, and a small refrigerator.

Many owner-operators became who they are by first working for corporations. They gave that up to gain freedom. Now, many of them are working for their trucks. So where's the freedom? I know that independent truckers are a proud lot. It's not easy to do what they do, and they deserve to be proud. But there's no pride in going out of business.

Now let's discuss the definition of the Brand's unique value proposition (the UVP).

CHAPTER 18

The Unique Value Proposition

Customers must recognize that you stand for something.
—*Howard Schultz, Starbucks*

Probably the most important sentence that a marketer could write about his or her brand would be the sentence that states the brand's unique value proposition or UVP. Unique Value Propositions, or UVPs, are, in effect, the epicenter of the brand story. Every step in the StoryBrief leads inescapably toward it, every marketing or operational action flows from it. With it, the brand has a reason for being; without it, the brand is aimless. The UVP is the point, the punch line, and the premise of the brand story all rolled up into a simple, provocative sentence. In other words, it's damn important.

The UVP is *the* unique belief that we want both employees and prospects to associate with the brand, beyond its functional purpose. It is purposefully brief because it should not need explanation. Rather, when stated, its meaning should be very clear to anyone associated with the brand.

The UVP explains the big "why" behind the brand, beyond its profit motive. A UVP might be stated as, "We believe in the value of invention that is responsive, not just for invention's sake," or "It's important to do things the hard way so that no stone is left unturned." As is sometimes the case, the UVP is not to be confused with its older and more familiar cousin, the USP, or unique selling proposition. As acronyms, UVP and USP may differ by just one letter, but in meaning, they are miles apart.

The USP was defined by Rosser Reeves. Reeves was an adman who worked for Ted Bates & Co., a leading advertising agency during the 1950s and 60s, the early days of TV advertising. By the time Reeves coined the term, TV advertising had reached adolescent wildness and was in need of reliable structure and discipline, something Reeves tried to provide in his book *Reality in Advertising*:

> Each advertisement must make a proposition to the consumer. Not just words, not just product puffery, not just show-window advertising. Each advertisement must say to each reader: "Buy this product, and you will get this specific benefit."
>
> The proposition must be one that the competition either cannot, or does not, offer. It must be unique—either a uniqueness of the brand or a claim not otherwise made in that particular field of advertising.
>
> The proposition must be so strong that it can move the mass millions (i.e., pull over new customers to your product).

On the other hand, and unlike the USP, a brand's UVP has nothing to do with describing what a brand does or how well it does relative to the competition. It extolls a belief, not a benefit. It is more about the brand's cause than its claim as it explains why the brand does what it does beyond its profit motive.

In story terms, the USP is most like the story's plot. The UVP is most like the story's theme. The plot of a story might be about the good guy struggling but finally prevailing to put the bad guy behind bars. In this case, the theme might be that persistence wins or that evil can't hide from virtue. The theme of any story is subject to the audience's interpretation, but it always imparts what its audience would consider a worthwhile maxim. The author's objective is to share what he or she sees as a truth, but, unlike the plot, it isn't told in the story; it's told through the story. The same can be said about UVPs. Unlike USPs that are told by the seller, UVPs are told through the selling because everything the brand does and how it performs demonstrates what the UVP is. Through this demonstration the consumer decides whether the brand is paying lip service to what it believes is important or if, in fact, it truly is important.

The UVP does not depend on the seller's assertions. It depends on the seller's motivation.

Assertions, regardless of facts that back them up, are still subject to scrutiny, argument, and for the cynics among us, constant doubt. This is not to suggest that facts do not matter. They do. However, as has been suggested throughout this book, facts alone won't matter as much as why those facts are being delivered.

Consider the used-car salesman who might approach you with a line like, "This car has more options per dollar than any other used car on our lot." Certainly, you are not going to do a cost/benefit analysis on each car in his lot. You only have to trust in him to determine if that fact is true. That trust may very well be minimized by the stigma associated with used-car salesmen. By contrast, consider the doctor who tells you that you need some important treatment. Chances are you will believe him or her. In fact, countless insurance studies have shown that the vast majority of patients do not seek out second opinions for doctor-prescribed treatments and will readily accept their doctor's assertion.

Perhaps the biggest difference between the used-car salesman and the doctor is a difference in relative source credibility. There can be no minimizing the importance of credibility. However, a fact is a fact, no matter how credible the source. As such, it can always be doubted or debated. The perceived motivation of the seller of those facts will always have a strong influence on whether or not those facts are seen as true. Enhancing perceived motivations is a function of a brand's UVP.

One strike against every brand's perceived motivation is selfish pursuit. Sellers of brands may try to convince prospects that they truly care about them, but we all know that how much they care is often a function of how much the prospect is willing to pay for that care. Unlike the USP, however, the purpose of the UVP is not to directly and outwardly try to convince the prospect of anything more than the assertion that the brand stands for the same important values and beliefs that he or she stands for.

THE UNIQUENESS PROBLEM

Often, two or more competitors within a category will be propelled by the same belief. The insurance category, for instance, is one where the belief in protecting others may be the brand's driving ambition. The way protection is offered may be somewhat unique, but the value proposition itself is nothing new.

When faced with this dilemma, the best story wins. Expression and evidence either add or subtract value. How well the value proposition resonates with the audience should be the ultimate test. This is perhaps more art than science, since subjectivity plays an important role.

However, as a rule, when comparing executions of the same belief, we place the emphasis on resonance. This can be measured in terms of the respondents' answers to questions that help gauge the extent to which the brand's truth is identified as one's own. For example, Is this brand for people like them? or How closely do they identify with what this brand is all about and why? Although these questions do not directly reflect whether one execution is liked over another, we work from the assumption that value identification wins on all fronts.

THEME LINES VS. PLOT LINES

I'm often asked if the UVP is just another name for the campaign's theme line or tagline. The answer is both yes and no. Sometimes it might be appropriate to adopt the UVP as the brand's theme line; other times not. In the case of Bleach Bright, the UVP of "Looking confident helps one feel confident," might be a little cumbersome creatively. There are undoubtedly more memorable ways to communicate the same thought, such as *Look Confident, Feel Confidence* or something as simple as *Look as bright as you feel.* You may come up with others that do a better job, but my purpose here is to advise you to let creative expression take a backseat to defining of the UVP first. Concentrate on the belief first, and worry about how it is stated later.

That said, and when the discussion gets to creative expressions, know the difference between what we refer to, respectively, as a theme line and a plot line.

Theme lines (or taglines) should imply the brand's belief the way a story's theme expresses the story's significance. Plot lines, on the other hand, express what the brand wants the prospect to believe. There is a big and important difference.

By virtue of the way they are stated, theme lines enlist subscription to specific human values or beliefs that are thought to be important. Drawing again from stories, a theme might be "Love makes the world go 'round," or "Crime doesn't pay." Although these aren't original, they are what we would constitute as themes simply because they imply subscription. In other words, they are intended as belief statements that resonate with people who share the belief they express. The implication is that they are important values.

Plot lines are what we typically see advertisers using. Plot lines explicate what the brand is and does from the brand's point of view. Their transparent purpose is to sell superiority. As such, they are expected and often discounted or resisted simply because they express the opinion of the seller. They have more to do with the product's USP than the brand's UVP.

For theme line examples, let's turn to some brands that are currently using them. For instance, when Apple ends its commercials with the phrase "Think Different," it is urging its audience to follow along with the notion that thinking unconventionally is important. The implication is that this belief is the guiding light that Apple follows and one that describes its intention. In effect, this theme describes what Apple stands for, while entreating subscription from those who share the belief.

Here are some other examples of theme lines that have been or are currently being used by prominent brands:

- Never Stop Exploring: North Face
- Be All That You Can Be: The Army
- Screw it! Let's Ride: Harley-Davidson
- You deserve a break today: McDonald's
- Just Do It!: Nike
- Yes we can!: Barack Obama
- A mind is a terrible thing to waste: United Negro College Fund

- Obey your thirst: Sprite
- Image is everything: Canon
- Make yourself heard: Erickson

We often refer to plot lines as *brag* lines, simply because that is what they do. They express the brand's *what* more than its *why* that was discussed in chapter 11. Plot lines are more a manifestation of the brand's opinion of itself. As such, they lack the believability and relevance of theme lines. And by themselves, they rarely make an emotional connection.

Consider the following plot lines:

- You're in good hands: Allstate Insurance
- Like a rock: Chevy Trucks
- It's the real thing: Coke
- Easy as Dell: Dell
- Your world delivered: AT&T
- Where the rubber meets the road: Firestone
- Ford has a better idea: Ford
- We bring good things to life: G.E.

One of the driving forces behind StoryBranding is that when resonance increases, resistance decreases. Theme lines increase resonance; plot lines increase resistance.

SOME USEFUL UVP THOUGHT-TRIGGERS

UVPs are very similar to lessons or morals that we learned as children from the likes of Aesop's fables, religious parables, and other stories passed on to us by parents and teachers. If you are having difficulty articulating your brand's UVP, reintroducing yourself to these lessons can be a very useful tool. Read through this list that I've compiled for you here. See if anything here resembles the belief or value that you most want associated with your brand. You may need to rework the language, but this list can serve as a good thought-starter. Other lists are available on the Internet.

- A fine appearance is a poor substitute for inward worth.
- A humble life with peace and quiet is better than a splendid one with danger and risk.
- A man is known by the company he keeps.
- An act of kindness is a good investment.
- Attempt not impossibilities.
- Avoid a remedy that is worse than the disease.
- Be on guard against people who can strike from a distance.
- Slow but steady wins the race.
- Beauty is only skin-deep.
- Birds of a feather flock together.
- The hero is brave in words as well as deeds.
- Pleasure bought with pain hurts.
- The best intentions do not always ensure success.
- Clothes do not make the man.
- Do not be in a hurry to change one evil for another.
- Whatever you do, do with all your might.
- The memory of a good deed lives.
- The more honor, the more danger.
- Counsel without help is useless.
- Count the cost before you commit yourselves.
- Do not attempt to hide things that cannot be hid.
- Do not attempt too much at once.
- Do not count your chickens before they are hatched.

- Do not try to do that which is not natural to you.
- Do nothing without a regard to the consequences.
- Even the wise must recognize their limits.
- Union is strength.
- Try before you trust.

Another great source that I contact regularly is www.brainyquote. com. Here you can look up quotes by topic or author. Again, surf through this site and see if anything triggers a thought about how best to state your UVP.

Again, and sad to say, most advertising we see is tagged with plot lines. The use of theme lines, in the truest sense of what a theme line is, is generally the exception more than the rule. Implication rather than explication is one of the most powerful lessons we can take away from stories.

Review

- The unique value proposition (UVP) is the statement that sums up the unique human value associated with a given brand, such as love, freedom, independence, or creativity.

- The UVP is not to be confused with its older and more familiar cousin, the USP, or unique selling proposition. In story terms, the UVP is the brand's theme, and the USP is the plot.

- The goal for writing a UVP is to create a simple yet emotionally provocative statement that uniquely sums up a belief that prospects will share.

- In writing the UVP, the objective is to powerfully communicate a shared belief in a way that is charged with emotion.

- There is a discernible and highly significant difference between a theme (UVP) and a plot line (USP). Plot lines are more a manifestation of the brand's opinion of itself.

- Plot lines explicate what the brand is and does from the brand's point of view. Their transparent purpose is to sell superiority.

- The difference between a theme line and a plot line is the difference between a story and an editorial.

- One of the driving forces behind StoryBranding is that as resonance increases, resistance decreases.

PART III

TELLING THE STORY

CHAPTER 19

Testing

The single biggest problem with communication is the
illusion that it has taken place.
—George Bernard Shaw

One of the underlying premises to this book is the notion that meaning
is not in words. It is in people. Miscommunication is often a function
of erroneously assuming that what you mean is going to be correctly
interpreted by your audience.

This explains why advertisers spend so much money testing what
they are going to say before they say it. Yet, I would contend, having
taken part in many communication tests over my thirty-plus years in
advertising, that the risk of miscommunication is sometimes facilitated
by the very tests that are used.

Many marketers have come to rely on focus groups, or groups of
people hired to sit around a table and discuss a given campaign, commercial, or concept. A trained moderator leads the discussion. Focus
groups provide a fast and economical source of respondent feedback.
However, they are often given far more validity than they deserve.

Focus groups, when originally devised, were seen as a form of "exploratory research," or research used to arrive at possible answers to questions. It is believed that discussions with a group of people will provide rich insights and help form hypotheses for later testing. This is based on the assumption that information extracted from a group is richer than information extracted from individuals. Much of this depends on the moderator, however. A good moderator might pose a controversial subject, inviting a debate. And through the give-and-take of that debate, he or she might be able to discern the various pros and cons surrounding a subject. Additionally, debates can often reveal how much emotional attachment might exist for certain brands from the positions that respondents take.

As an exploratory tool, focus groups can provide many possible answers to questions and/or lead to questions that haven't been asked. But oftentimes, in fact too often, focus groups are given far more reliability and validity than they deserve. There are too few people interviewed and too many dynamics at work in focus groups to definitively prove anything. Some people don't like to debate or publicly disagree with others in a group setting. There might be, and often is, one person who will dominate the discussion and have a strong influence on others. These are just some of the inherent drawbacks that make focus groups more exploratory than definitive.

If the purpose of the research is to provide definitive answers to questions, then using a focus group is like using a can opener to uncork a bottle of wine.

On the other hand, survey research or any form of research that uses large numbers in its sample will present drawbacks as well. One of the problems we run into is reliability of the answers. I may ask a sizeable sample to please indicate whether this is a long or short sentence. Each respondent is asked to circle one of two words to indicate their answer: long or short. Fifty-five percent may answer "long" while 45% may answer "short." Because this was a forced-choice question, this question pushes anyone who doesn't think it is either long nor short toward one of two polar opposites. This may be done on purpose to eliminate the middle and to see how people may be leaning. But ask them again tomorrow. Because many might be uncertain, they may answer differently.

Another problem is that conclusions drawn may be invalid. In the case above, I might conclude that most people will consider a seventeen-word sentence to be a "long" sentence. Not accounting for the fact that the sample size may not be big enough such that there is any statistically significant difference between 55% and 45%, and that no other seventeen-word sentences were compared, this conclusion may be completely invalid. Furthermore, the survey doesn't help anyone understand when long is too long.

Many of the issues surrounding survey research can be dealt with by a skilled research specialist and through proper questionnaire design. But even the best of them will tell you that there's no guarantee that anything coming out of what is referred to as "quantitative research" is definitive.

Research, in general, is an aid to judgment. Depending on the type of research, the aid can vary between strong and weak. And often that comes down to judgment as well. This is in no way an indictment of research. But I think the most important lesson I can provide from my years of experience working with research can be summed up in one word: Beware.

RESONANCE DEVELOPMENT TESTING (RDT)

The day that some form of research is developed that provides an absolute predictor of success in determining the best way to stage a brand's identity is the day when computers come with beating hearts. That said, we have come across one technique that can lead to a number of great insights. In the end, however, and to restate the theme of this chapter, when it comes to any form of research, there can no be substitute for good judgment.

The technique is something we call a Resonance Development Test (RDT). It is a technique that can employ both exploratory and quantitative research, depending on budgets. It can be performed using one-on-one interviews with respondents to eliminate group dynamic problems that sometimes confound focus group results. Additionally, and if budgets permit, surveys with larger samples can be conducted. Many Internet research services are available that can do this.

The purpose of the test is to evolve the best match between alternative brand and prospect I AM statements with the help of respondents. I liken this to the game of "hot and cold" that we played as kids. By getting feedback from respondents as to whether or not the information you provide is either hot or cold, you can start to form better judgments about what will work best.

Using the necessary screening criteria, we hand or send out alternative I AM statements that have been written for both the prospect and the brand. We then ask respondents to circle the sentences that especially appeal to them, while crossing out those statements that, for one reason or another, they do not like. What remains are considered to be the neutral sentences. If a focus group is used, and after this initial exercise, we go around the group polling what was liked and disliked. Then, and only then, do we discuss the *whys* behind their answers. Keep in mind that what you will receive is not definitive since your sample is so small.

We then look for dramatic similarities between people. During one-on-one interviews or focus groups, we study body language to determine the importance or relative unimportance of the feedback being provided. Again, we don't draw absolute conclusions. We merely use what we learn to generate or negate hypotheses.

Finally, we provide a list of different UVPs and once again ask for individuals to rate them in terms of whether or not they express a belief that is shared. We make it very clear that we are not interested in opinions about how clever or memorable the line is, so we can avoid turning the group into copywriters.

In one case, we had written an I AM statement for the prospect of a fast-casual restaurant. This restaurant, like most fast-casual restaurants, serves a more varied menu at higher price-points than traditional fast-food restaurants like McDonald's and Burger King. In the I AM statement for the prospect, we stated the following: "I don't frequent fast-food restaurants as much as I used to."

When we collected the respondents' reactions to our I AM statements, we noticed that this statement was circled by everyone as being a statement they liked. In turn, we asked respondents to tell us why they liked this statement. The respondents told us that fast-food employees are less service-oriented. People became very animated as that stated things like, "People who work in fast-food restaurants don't really care about my satisfaction," "Fast-food people are generally rude or careless," or "When I go to a fast-casual restaurant like (example given), people are usually more friendly and more upbeat." One person said, "I feel more pampered when I go to (example given)." This led us to revise the I AM statement to emphasize an important expectation prospects might have for restaurants that categorize themselves as fast and casual.

In the I AM statement for the brand, we also included the following statement: "I am mindful of the need for sandwich variety."

Most of the respondents crossed out this statement. When probed, the consensus was that being "mindful" was not good enough. Prospects wanted proof, so we revised the statement with specific examples that gave prospects the proof they needed.

We might give prospects three or four UVP statements to choose from. Surveying the likes and the dislikes helps us to zero in on the most resonant UVPs. Further investigating with *why* questions, we are able to pinpoint possible reasons for their choice. Depending on the number of respondents we used this technique with, and the difference between the UVPs we test, we typically walk away with a stronger basis for choosing one over another.

The choice is yours as to how many times you test, revise, and test again. A good qualitative research moderator will help arrive at the salient sentences, words, or phrases that resonate in addition to those that need to be eliminated or revised to avoid negative reactions.

Again, the purpose of Resonance Development is to "develop" or evolve both brand and prospect I AM statements as well as the UVP into something that we believe will have a good chance of success.

Resonance Development Testing is not the *be-all and end-all* research technique, by any means. However, as an adjunct to the StoryBranding process, it makes use of the work that has been done up to the completion of the Story Brief. If you have any doubts about how this or any research should be conducted, I strongly recommended that you spend the necessary money to hire a skilled research analyst. It's like buying an insurance policy that can help make certain you are not making any of the common mistakes associated with communications research.

Review

- The risk of miscommunication is sometimes facilitated by the very tests that are used to measure communication effectiveness.

- As an exploratory tool, focus groups can provide many possible answers to questions and/or lead to questions that haven't been asked. But oftentimes, in fact too often, focus groups are given far more reliability and validity than they deserve.

- Survey research, or any form of research that uses large numbers in its sample, will present drawbacks as well.

- Research, in general, is an aid to judgment.

- The purpose of the Resonance Development Test (RDT) is to evolve the most resonant I AM statements for both the brand and prospect.

- We ask respondents to circle the sentences that especially appeal to them while crossing out those statements that they do not like.

- We provide a list of different UVPs and, once again, ask for individuals to rate them in terms of whether or not they express a shared belief.

CHAPTER 20

Big-T vs. Small-t Truth

What happens is fact, not truth. Truth is what we think about what happens.
—*Robert McKee, Story*

Once the Story Brief, including I AM statements and the UVP, have been written and perhaps tested, the messaging process begins, and all marketing communication elements are created. There's no magic formula or black box prescription to message creation. Whereas we do prefer the creative technique of story*telling*, we realize it is not always practical, especially when we're working with media that require very short messages. As for other techniques, all options are always on the table.

We have one principle, however, that we adhere to no matter what creative technique we've employed. As we've alluded to throughout this book, successful story writers subscribe to the same principle. It is a belief that truth is not what is said, but what is believed.

TRUTH IN STORIES

As we discussed throughout this book, stories don't create our beliefs. Rather, their themes are like magnets that find and attach themselves to beliefs that already exist. Additionally, the best stories amplify the importance of existing beliefs by charging them with emotion. Telling someone that war sucks conveys information. Showing someone how war destroys the hopes and dreams of innocent people conveys the same information with power.

Additionally, stories provide an easily digested context for truth. Logan Pearsall Smith, the American essayist, once said, "What I like in a good author is not what he says, but what he whispers." Because stories do not outwardly profess or directly tell us how to think and feel, we welcome their points of view. As we've demonstrated earlier, when resonance increases, resistance decreases. This principle has far-reaching implications for marketing communications in general, particularly when it comes to advertising.

TRUTH IN ADVERTISING

An oft-quoted statement attributed to the late Bill Bernbach, founder of Doyle Dane Bernbach, is that "the best advertising tells the truth." However, and with due respect for a man who has inspired and created so much great advertising, I've always had a hard time with this quote. I can only guess at what he meant by "truth."

The movie *Crazy People* is one of several that parody the advertising business. It's about an advertising agency that sets out to sell honesty. In turn, it creates ads with headlines such as "Volvo. They're boxy but they're safe," or "Don't mess with AT&T. We're all you've got." For some reason, I don't think this is the truth that Bill Bernbach was referring to. So what did he mean?

Truth is an abstraction that philosophers have grappled with as far back as we can trace thought. Whatever the definition of truth is, or could be, we all know what our individual truths are. These are what provide the engines for many, if not most, of our behaviors. Considering this, perhaps what Bernbach really meant was that the best advertising tells us something consumers believe is true for themselves. This would seem to make sense. It makes even more sense considering the effect stories have on us.

BIG-T AND SMALL-T TRUTH

The concept of Big-T vs. small-t truth is not my invention. In fact, if you read only a small percentage of the suggested further readings listed in the appendix, you'll run into a number of references to this concept. Different writers describe it differently. But I particularly gravitate to the description that Robert McKee provides in his book, *Story*, considered by many to be the bible of screenwriting:

> Fact, no matter how minutely observed, is truth with a small 't.' Big 'T' Truth is located behind, beyond, inside, below the surface of things, holding reality together or tearing it apart, and cannot be directly observed.

Small-t truth is objective, is either provable fact or arguable opinion. It appeals to the rational side of our brains. It typically comes at us from others who want us to know what they want us to know. Small-t truths are explicitly stated and directly communicated. In stories, they might consist of details used to describe a character or an event. For example, "The young boy felt intimidated playing chess with men three times his age," or "The circus was something everyone looked forward to each year." They are the facts that a story is built upon.

In advertising, small-t truths are explicitly stated. Small-t truths are found in statements like "The number-one selling sprocket in the United States," or "Mega Bright makes your teeth whiter." Besides being provable or refutable facts, small-t truths in advertising often express arguable opinions, too: "You'll feel secure knowing you're protected by Acme Alarms" or "You'll save big during our holiday sale." The brand's outer layer is comprised of small-t truths.

On the other hand, Big-T Truths appeal to the nonrational side of our brains, where they are often colored by and linked to some emotion. Rather than coming at us, Big-T Truths come from within us. They contain our interpretations of what we're being told. We may learn small-t truths from description, but we *know* Big-T Truths from our personal perceptions and beliefs.

A great and instructive parallel is evident here for creating advertising messages. If your brand advertising claims that your brand is faster, cheaper, or more long-lasting, you are dealing in the realm of arguable and refutable truth. This may be necessary when trying to create a Level I or even a Level II connection. But it should be understood that small-t truths have major limitations. First, they have expiration dates, because competitors will soon copy them. And second, they are met with some resistance because they make the sales motive transparent.

Big-T Truths are sometimes difficult to articulate and often have to be inferred from the way we feel. "I feel scared" suggests an underlying Big-T Truth that is triggered through identification with the source of the fear. It can be triggered by beliefs, rational or irrational, such as "airplanes are unsafe" or "the stock market is a bad place to invest money." This is one of the reasons why psychologists typically try to engage their patients in talking about their feelings. Feelings are the windows to Big-T Truths.

Big-T Truths do not always have to be communicated through words. Much of our communication is nonverbal. Production values, gestures, symbols, and other unspoken elements of an ad or commercial can often say more than words. In fact, we've been known to create highly effective commercials without words—just visuals followed by a logo and a theme. What this communicates to the audience is a respect for their intelligence—something often lacking in today's advertising.

This, I think, is probably one of the most important ideas to consider before putting pencil to paper or fingers to keyboards when creating advertising. Too often, we see advertisers talking more to themselves than to their audiences. They may believe that their brand makes people smile or makes them feel secure, smart, or fashionable, all the time ignoring the most important feeling people desire: the feeling of being understood. The most powerful advertising is advertising that generates a "that's me or my problem they're talking about" response. This, I believe, tops the list of important lessons that can be drawn from the art of storytelling.

Review

- Stories don't create our beliefs. Rather, their themes are like magnets that find and attach themselves to beliefs that already exist.

- This principle has far-reaching implications for marketing communications in general, particularly when it comes to advertising.

- Whatever the definition of truth is, or could be, we all know what our individual truths are.

- Small-t truth typically comes at us from others who want us to know what they want us to know.

- Big-T Truths appeal to the nonrational side of our brains where they are often colored by and linked to some emotion. Rather than coming at us, Big-T Truths come from within us.

- The most powerful advertising is advertising that generates a "that's me or my problem they're talking about" response.

CHAPTER 21

The Care and Feeding of the Creative Animal

If your actions inspire others to dream more, learn more,
and become more, you are a leader.
—John Quincy Adams

I've spent my entire career on the agency side of the marketing communications business. A great deal has changed during these past thirty-plus years. But one thing, unfortunately, remains the same. It has to do with the way clients and agency personnel alike generally utilize creative talent.

Many people are responsible for the success of a brand. But few have as much to do with the way a brand is projected to consumers as the creative team in charge of a brand's message. And when it comes to that task, a lot is on the line. Perhaps this explains, in part, why creative people are sometimes micromanaged by fearful clients and account people with direction that includes everything from the rewritten headlines to copy and/or a drawn layout. Unfortunately this happens often enough that creatives have coined the phrase *being wristed* to describe how this behavior makes them feel.

I am not suggesting that those who are referred to as the creatives are the only creative people associated with a brand. They are most definitely not. However, these are people who spend the greater part of their day creating word and picture combinations that communicate to consumers. Many have a great deal of experience and are constantly on the lookout for ways to up their messaging skills. If you have any doubts about that, sit through a TV show with a writer or an art director. The best among them are not people who will readily fast forward through commercials. Instead they watch while asking themselves, "How could I have done it better?"

Creatives are not infallible. But they do have experienced judgment that is the result of their specialization. The best way to take advantage of that specialization is to inspire their output rather than dictate it. In my experience, I have found that the best creative people are synthesizers. They are like super-absorbent sponges taking in tons of information from their senses. Then, after combining that information with the storehouse of information already packed away in their heads, *presto change-o*: new ways of seeing things are born. How creatives arrive at good ideas is a function of many uncontrollable factors. But as the people in charge of planning the brand story, there is one factor that we can and must control: the information we give them from the start.

A current that has run through this book is the notion that creatives must be inspired to do their best work. Inspiration goes beyond giving the facts. It includes a nonrational, felt-more-than-explicated engagement with the reasons behind the facts. The best creative direction includes involvement and immersion—something a data dump can't provide. Creatives do their best work when their senses are enlivened, when they see and feel for themselves what the prospect sees and feels, and when the brand is something they experience, the same way they would experience another human being.

Yes, certain objectives must be accomplished, but too often in an effort to make sure that the creative output achieves its goal, emphasis is placed on what should or shouldn't be considered or, worse yet, said. Instead, when we provide creative input, we do it with more emphasis given to what will inspire original thinking than contain or constrict it. For some this is uncomfortable, as a certain amount of control has to be given up. Fear of not getting what is needed creeps into creative briefs with statements such as "the tonality of the message should be humorous," or "we need more appetizing descriptors of the food." But, as we've seen time and time again, the best thinking is usually the product of freedom. I AM statements allow that freedom, as they favor interpretive over regulated thinking. They do not provide the do's and don'ts. Rather they leave it up to the creative team to naturally arrive at what's most important to be communicated as well as how it can best be communicated.

Review

- Many people are responsible for the success of a brand. But few have as much to do with the way a brand is projected to consumers as the creative team in charge of a brand's message.

- Many creatives have a great deal of experience and are constantly on the lookout for ways to up their messaging skills.

- Creatives do their best work when their senses are enlivened, when they see and feel for themselves what the prospect sees and feels, and when the brand is something they experience, the same way they would experience another human being.

- As the people in charge of planning the brand story, there is one factor that we can and must control: the information we give them from the start.

CHAPTER 22

Sell the Truth

Storytelling reveals meaning without committing the error of defining it.
—Hannah Arendt, political theorist

The two words at the end of every story tell the audience where the story stops. These two words signal the time when the author's voice stops and our inner voice begins. For that reason, *The End* is more of a beginning. It invites the audience to put the story into their own personal perspective, deciding on its relevance and personal meaning.

This is The End to my story. Having presented the case for approaching brands as stories, it is now up to you to decide on how that can be done. For some, StoryBranding is a radical departure from traditional marketing and communication planning processes. For others, it is a natural extension of what has gone before it. My hope is that, at the very least, it has provided a new perspective that can help marketing communicators draw on one of the oldest persuasive tools known to mankind.

I've often wondered why, after thirty years in the advertising and marketing business, I discovered the benefit of seeing brands as stories.

Perhaps it is because I've been too hard-headed to see something that was staring me in the face just waiting to be discovered. Perhaps it is because I was blinded by too many rules that led me astray from the importance of simply selling the truth. I'm not sure, nor do I think I'll ever be sure.

But this much I do know. Seeing brands as stories has opened me up to following new routes to similar destinations and new destinations that could not have been found otherwise. I've come to appreciate what brands really are beyond the typical textbook definitions.

It is only fitting that I end this book on StoryBranding with a story. What follows is a Hasidic folk tale, and one that best summarizes one of the most important lessons I've learned about selling the truth.

Naked Truth, wrapped in Story's robes

Truth walked naked into a village, and almost immediately the local inhabitants started cursing at him. Spewing epithets, they chased him out of the village, and Truth walked along the road to the next town. But they, too, spit at him, cursed him, and spewed epithets, driving him out of that town as well.

He walked, lonely and sad, along the empty road until he reached the next town, still hoping to find someone who was happy to see him, who would embrace naked Truth with open arms.

So he walked into the third town, this time in the middle of the night, hoping that the morning would find the townsfolk happy to see Truth in the clear light of dawn. But as soon as the townsfolk's eyes lit upon him, they ran to their homes and then came back throwing garbage at him.

Truth ran off out of the town and into the woods crying. After cleaning off the garbage, he returned to the edge of the woods, when he heard laughter and gaiety, singing and applause. He saw the towns-folk applauding as Story entered the town. They brought out fresh meats and soups and pies and pastries and offered them all to Story—who smiled and reveled in their love and appreciation.

Come twilight, Truth was sulking and sobbing at the edge of the woods. The townsfolk disdainfully ignored him, but Story came out to meet Truth on the edge of town.

Truth told Story how the folk of every town mistreated him, how sad and lonely he was, and how much he wanted to be accepted and appreciated.

Story replied, "Of course they all reject you!" Story looked at Truth, eyes a bit lowered to the side. "No one ever wants to look at the naked Truth."

So Story took pity on Truth and gave him some of her colorful, beautiful clothing to wear. Then they walked into the nearby town together, Truth dressed in the beautiful robes of Story. The towns-people greeted them with warmth and love and appreciation, for Truth wrapped in Story's clothing can be a beautiful thing, and is almost always easier to behold. Truth as Story allowed listeners to come to their own conclusions.

And ever since that day, Truth has traveled best with Story, and when Truth is wrapped in Story's robes, he finds much more accep-tance than the simple naked Truth would ever find.

CHAPTER 23

Oh, One More Thing

I think of Steve Jobs as probably the greatest marketer of all time. And in honor and remembrance of him, I've decided to conclude this book in a way that he would end his iconic keynotes. Instead of making concluding remarks, Steve would start to walk off stage then turn back to say, "Oh, there's one more thing." Feigned as an afterthought, his "one more thing" would always turn out to be something significant.

Since StoryBranding was first published, I've had the fortunate privilege of speaking in front of groups on the subject and how brand marketers can benefit from the process. Typically during the Q&A, I'm asked if any of the StoryBranding principles discussed in this book can be applied to personal branding and/or sales. The answer is an emphatic "yes." As a matter of fact, I am currently working on planning models that could become the foundation of a separate book at some later date.

In the meantime, here are some thoughts and tips that you will hopefully find helpful.

STORYBRANDING FOR PERSONAL BRANDING

As was pointed out earlier, if you have a birth certificate, you are a brand. Your name accumulates associations just as any brand name does. And as a brand, you have an outer and an inner layer.

Your outer layer consists of what you tell others about what you do and how you do it. It includes your accomplishments, experience, your professional objectives, etc. Unfortunately, this is where most attempts to shape a personal brand start and stop. See for yourself. Just peruse a sampling of LinkedIn profiles. The vast majority will provide self-described facts and opinions, with a few third-party testimonials and/or recommendations thrown in for good measure.

For you, this should spell opportunity. Right this very minute, you can help your profile, or any self-description of your personal brand, stand out against the typical self-description by finding, creating, and revealing your inner layer. Here are some thoughts on how to do it:

Tell a personal story relevant to why you chose your profession. When I interview candidates for our agency, I always ask the question, "Why did you decide to go into advertising?" Typically I get well-rehearsed answers like, "Advertising requires both right-brain and left-brain thinking; I'm good at both," "I think my biggest strength is creativity," or "You get to work on a variety of businesses."

Yet this question provides a huge opportunity to tell a personal story and one that reflects who you are as a person. One of the best ways to stand out is to tell a personal story that addresses your career decision. Don't shy away from ways to reflect your personality. Profiles don't have to be completely dry and factual. Use humor, be conversational, or be self-deprecating to show that you are a living, breathing person behind those credentials.

Try to avoid directly telling your audience what you believe in or value. Rather, imply beliefs and values instead. For instance, highlight a favorite quote and explain why you like the quote. I sometimes draw on my favorite quote by saying, "Someone once told me that stories persuade without getting in their own way." Look for quotes that resonate with you, and draw on them as a way to imply what you stand for. Do this when writing or speaking about yourself in profiles, blogs, job interviews, or any time or place where you are asked to describe yourself.

Be modest. Certainly your credentials will say a great deal about your accomplishments. Rather than listing what you've done, explain how your experience has helped you, and always sound grateful. You might say something like, "Right out of college, I got lucky. I was one of two college graduates hired to the HP training program. There I learned about the importance of _____." Reflect your values and beliefs by talking about the things you learned from some or all of those experiences, e.g., "While working for P&G, I learned about the importance of _____."

Say something about your personal life that colors the picture of who you are outside of work. "I'm an obsessive PEZ collector." "When I'm not working, I'm actively involved in mentoring high school kids through Junior Achievement. I see this as an opportunity to help deserving kids become productive adults."

Add a call to action if you can. If you've written an article, given a speech, created a photo board that tells your life story in pictures . . . drive your audience to it in order for them to learn more about who you are and what makes you tick.

In sum, just as with any brand, the way to reveal your inner layer is to rely on *show* more than *tell*. Demonstrate, elucidate, and allow your audience to get inside your head and your heart. Help them to see for themselves what you stand for.

FOR SALES

Invite your prospect to tell you about their story. Tell them that you'd like to learn a little more about them. Then ask them to tell you something that engages their passion. "I'm just curious; I read that you were the person behind Brand X's revival. What was the insight that triggered the positive change?" Or, "Why did you decide to move over from operations to marketing?" Just make sure you ask an open-ended question or something that will give your prospect a chance to talk. While your prospect is answering your question, listen for values and beliefs. Use your questions to understand him or her as a person, not just a buyer.

Know your brand's story. Go beyond the facts that make your brand better than the competitor's alternative. Know what your brand believes in and what it stands for, and show how that's been demonstrated. It's one thing to tell your prospect that you have a guarantee. It's another to suggest to your prospect that your company believes in its product performance such that they feel very little risk in offering a five-year guarantee.

Think about the obstacles as identified in chapter 14. Remember that the ultimate goal is to get to Level IV, where a strong relationship becomes the motivating force behind the sale. And remember that relationships are formed on the basis of shared beliefs and values. Know what those shared beliefs and values are between you, your brand, your prospect, and his/her brand.

Use I AM statements to help you better understand your prospects. Write what you assume to be true about their inner and outer layers. Use this tool as a way to immerse yourself in your prospect's world while articulating what you think his or her obstacles are as well as how you and your brand can help overcome them.

Know the difference between a case history and a story. A case history merely states the facts about what happened. A story includes some conflict or obstacle that had to be overcome. Dramatize the obstacle and show how your brand helped a specific customer with a solution.

Use colorful language. Metaphors, similes, and analogies can paint pictures in the mind that facts can't. A salesman once started his pitch by apologizing for having to postpone our first appointment. He could have said, "I'm sorry for taking so long to see you, but things have been a little crazy lately." Instead he told me that he had been "busier than a long-tail cat in a room full of rocking chairs." My initial thought was, "This guy is going to be interesting."

Finally, don't limit yourself to reading only nonfiction books, like this one. In order to fully appreciate the persuasive power of stories, read stories. Develop an appreciation for how they impact you and why. Try to discern the main character's inner layer, his or her motivating beliefs and values. See how novelists sell their points of view. Do this, and you will understand the process of StoryBranding better than any explanation I, or anyone else, could possibly provide.

Good luck and good StoryBranding.

PART IV

Essays on StoryBranding

—By Jim Signorelli as they have appeared on blog.eswstorylab.com

BRANDS DON'T TRAVEL AS FAR AS STORIES

By the late sixties, Xerox had risen to become a highly successful global brand. Having a Xerox machine in the office had become a necessity. Now, with a well-established name, they decided to cultivate other ambitions. Xerox wanted to get into computer technology and data processing. It spent many years and millions of dollars before it finally threw in the towel.

It should come as no surprise that once a brand is strongly associated with a certain product, it is difficult, if not impossible, to change perceptions. Yet marketing history is rife with examples of companies expecting their well-established brand names to help them introduce new products.

Chiquita had to admit defeat after trying to convince us that Chiquita stood for more than bananas. Country Time Lemonade was forced to stop trying to sell Country Time Apple Cider. Ponds barely got out of the starting gates with Ponds toothpaste before it quit. Thousands of stories like these are out there.

But one could argue that Apple is proving to be the exception, as it has gone from a brand of computers to a brand of phones, iPads, TVs, and who-knows-what's next. Nike is yet another exception, as it has grown from making running shoes to becoming a successful seller of athletic equipment and apparel. And Branson keeps adding to the list of products which his brand Virgin is helping make successful. How does this happen?

It happens because Apple has never been just a company selling computers, Nike has never been simply about selling running shoes, and Virgin can sell pretty much anything it wants to. Why? Because they aren't selling brands. They are selling stories.

A brand has one layer; a brand story has two. Both have outer layers consisting of functional benefits or the results that can be achieved by using a given product. However, the brand story has an additional inner layer that gives it distance and longevity. It's like the golf ball's compacted core that keeps it in the air longer than a tennis ball when hit. The brand story's inner layer is more than just air. It's made up of very real values and beliefs.

When we buy brands, we buy products differentiated by function. When we buy brands that have become stories, we buy relatable and important meanings.

If your brand is nothing more than an outer layer, no doubt, growth has an expiration date. The good news is that it's never too late to find and communicate your brand's meaning, perhaps something Xerox should have thought about before trying to sell computers. That said, some challenges must be met:

First, your inner layer must be authentic. It's one thing for your brand's inner layer to be associated with the value of 'wow service.' But that value is quickly devalued when a customer is put on hold for twenty minutes while waiting to talk with customer service. It's one thing for your brand's inner layer to be associated with the value of simplicity, yet another when your customer is presented with too many buying restrictions. What you believe and what you do must be inextricably linked. Keep in mind that the truth behind your brand story is constantly being scrutinized via social media. Your truth must therefore be demonstrated and reinforced through every point of contact. Inconsistency is the bane of authenticity.

Second, audiences don't care what you think your inner layer is.

They care about what they think it is. Unlike outer layers, inner layers are more a function of what your audience sees for themselves as opposed to what you tell them to see. When we purchase a given brand, in effect we are hiring it. How much credence would you put in a job candidate who proclaims, "I believe in teamwork," or "I value hard work"? It's not enough to be told what someone believes. That belief must be shown or demonstrated.

Too often, we see advertising tag lines like "Excellence is all around you," or "Where service matters." However, the best brands don't get in their own way with brag and boast statements of self-description. Instead, they communicate their inner layers through mantras like "Think Different" or "Just Do It" or "Never Stop Exploring," ideals that resonate with existing beliefs that their audiences share. These are more than just tag lines. They are true theme lines that speak to the significance of their brands' stories.

Your brand must solve problems and provide opportunities. But if all you're doing is telling prospects about what your product does and/or how it does it better than similar products, you are telling them a story that is all plot with no important theme. To stand out as special, your brand must complete the story with the consistent proof of your brand's belief system. Every product then becomes a new chapter, a bigger story. Think story, not brand or product, and you'll last longer and go further.

FIVE WAYS TO TURN UP THE VOLUME OF YOUR BRAND'S AUTHENTIC STORY

Finding your authentic story is not a luxury for the touchy-feely. Given our overloaded channels of communication and the general lack of trust (and boredom) with advertising messages, finding your brand's true emotional core as expressed through its story is a must.

But first, you must know what you're looking for. Don't look to your elevator speech or your unique selling proposition. Your authentic story isn't there. Your elevator speech may take you one floor up while you tell prospects about functional differences that make your brand unique. But your key to the higher floors is in your authentic story, your belief, your cause, or some human value with which you want to be associated. And if presented in a way that will emotionally resonate with your prospects' worldview, and if you can walk the walk, short-term purchasers are bound to morph into brand evangelists.

Underneath those boastful sales claims, those self-descriptive tag lines, and that overly logical reason-why copy, a genuine and compelling brand story probably sits waiting to turn customers into joiners. Lying dormant, it also wants to provide your entire organization with an obvious way to discern right from wrong, good from bad, and relevant from irrelevant.

To find, claim, and clarify your authentic brand story, you must first look inside the heart of your brand. It can't be fabricated by its head. Chances are it's beating below the noise of all those meaningless facts that have been given a higher priority in your messaging. If you can't hear it yet, following are five ways to turn up the volume.

1. Ladder up

Start with the most important functional outcome that your product or service delivers: time and/or money savings, ease of use, or greater security. Then consider the underlying value associated with that functional benefit, e.g., freedom, simplicity, or safety. A way to get at this is to ask yourself why the functional outcome your brand delivers is important. Then ask again, why is that important? Keep asking why until you get to a human value (inventiveness, love, peace of mind, relaxation, etc.) that your brand supports above all else. Once you've landed on it, then ask yourself how you can go about owning it.

2. What your story isn't

Another way to get at your story is to decide on what its opposite is. If you were to do things the wrong way, what would that look like? What do you value least? What is the last thing you'd want your brand to be associated with? Oftentimes it's easier to describe what your purpose isn't to help you better define what it is.

3. Describe the enemy

Think of the enemy that your brand is setting out to overcome, e.g., time waste, stress, slow response time, etc. Then start to develop your enemy character. Describe what your enemy values most and what you value least. Sometimes a road paved with what you don't believe in will lead you to a place where you belong.

4. Find a role model story character

Think of your brand as a story character. Many books are available that describe brand archetypes that your brand might be best associated with (the caregiver, the maverick, the wise man, etc.). If you don't have access to these, try to identify a story hero that your brand is most like, and explain *why* in terms of *what* that hero values as important. But know the difference between what they do and why they do it. For example, Superman's purpose was not to jump tall buildings in a single bound. It was to protect the American way.

5. Get feedback from customers and employees

Ask customers and employees what they think you value most. Often-times, they will interpret your purpose based on their experience with yours and competitive brands. You'll either gain clarity or more reasons why you need to better tell your story.

I don't pretend this is an easy exercise. And it's not something that can always be discovered in a flash moment. Stay with it until you can see, hear, and feel your brand's authentic story. Your excavation will be well rewarded.

FIVE THINGS MARKETERS CAN LEARN FROM STORYTELLERS

Stories are one of the most powerful tools in our communication arsenal. Since the beginning of language, they continue to teach, inspire, motivate, and engage us like no other form of communication can. I've yet to see an audience give a standing O to a pie chart or go to the movies to watch a presentation of random, disconnected facts.

Many of the answers to why stories work the way they do are revealed to us by studying how storytellers of all kinds commonly go about their craft. It just so happens that a number of parallels exist between what storytellers do and what marketers can do to build magnetic brand identities. Here are five of my favorites:

1. Storytellers clothe facts with Big-M Meaning

All stories have meaning or some reason for being told. Consider this story:

The young athlete who trained by doing one hundred leg squats every day ended up first among one thousand runners.

In effect, this is a story about the functional benefit of leg squats for runners.

Now, consider this revision:

The young athlete, who trained by doing one hundred leg squats every day, ended up first among one thousand runners. He has a prosthetic leg.

The first story has what I call small-m meaning. It provides information that may be useful to its runner targets. However, the second story is more than just useful. It's inspirational. By contrast, it has Big-M Meaning. The additional five-word sentence makes the second story about the same runner far more significant.

Brand marketers need to ask how their brand can be made more inspiring or aspiring. Facts about unique features and benefits won't get you there. For Big-M Meaning to occur, your brand needs to be readily associated with a bigger personal value, e.g., exploration, perseverance, hard work, creativity. And that Big-M Meaning has to be expressed in an engaging way.

2. To engage their audiences, storytellers leave the thinking to us

Andrew Stanton, the creator of *Toy Story* and *Wall-E*, refers to his "unifying theory of 2+2" as our desire to come to our own conclusions. We do not want to be told the answer is 4. We'd rather figure it out for ourselves. This is one of the principles of story that attracts us to them as a communication device. Movies, novels, poems, or songs do not explain the meaning behind their messages. Meaning is left to the audience's interpretation.

This is very unlike advertising for brands that often gets in its own way. By telling us what meanings to associate with brands, we often resist or put up our protective BS shields. Consumers don't need or want to be told your brand is the one that cares most, works hardest, or thinks best.

Taking a lesson from the storyteller, it is far more engaging and believable to pull from the mind of the consumer than to push from the voice of the brand. Notice that in the second story above was no mention of what to think or feel. If you thought or felt anything about the runner with the prosthetic leg, it was because of your interpretation, not mine. Storytellers cause you to see what you see, but do little to cause the way you think or feel about what you see. Doing so would be like the comedian who explained the punch line of his joke. He doesn't get to do that twice.

3. Storytellers define their themes before developing their plots

Before a storyteller develops a story, he or she either consciously or unconsciously decides the story's reason for being or the point that needs to be made. Storytellers don't start creating the action within a plot and hope that it will somehow result in a meaningful story. In addition to providing clear direction for their writing, a theme-first approach gives storytellers the freedom to include twists and turns or to develop subplots that keep us engaged along the pathway to their main point.

Oftentimes brands will put plots before themes. For brands, the main point, or their overarching theme, is often an afterthought or very shallow. Brand meanings are often made up of well-recognized product features and unique functional benefits. This sets up a major stumbling block, as it is tantamount to writing the plot before arriving at an important theme. Because the brand's direction becomes too closely aligned with its current product, the brand's identity often needs to be changed in order to survive. Burger King built its brand around what was once the unique benefit of flame broiling. Today, it struggles to remain a viable contender within a very dynamic category where flame broiling is no longer a big deal. Midas Mufflers positioned itself as the muffler replacement expert. But then original equipment manufacturers discovered that stainless steel lasts longer, causing Midas to rethink its "Where we goin'?" Kodak became the first name in photographic film. Happy with achieving that goal, they didn't look long and hard enough to see the digital buzzkill in their future. Now contrast those brands with brands like Nike, Harley, Southwest Airlines, Apple, Disney, and Google. Brands like these are free to think more about growth than survival because their identities are not limited to a close association with a single product or functional benefit, or plot. Risk is spread over the rich meaning they built and one that can be made manifest through many new and related product and service initiatives.

4. Storytellers don't use focus groups to decide what their point-of-view is

Storytellers don't manufacture meaning on the basis of what will sell to the greatest number of people. Rather, they start with an authentically held core belief that needs expression.

Lack of authenticity is one of the many reasons why consumers have become cynical about advertising. Today's consumer is just too smart to fall for disingenuous claims designed solely for the purpose of winning more favor. They want and need brands to be in touch with their own truth first before attempting to be what research tells them they should be. And for them, the brand's truth will always be revealed more through actions than anything a brand says about itself. Trustable people don't tell you they are trustable.

If brands are to test anything, they should test ways to better communicate what they stand for, not what they should stand for.

5. Great storytellers always give us something to look forward to

If you go to any bestseller list of books, you'll often find that it consists of books written by authors with whom we are already familiar. This is largely due to the fact that we expect their new book to be a story told through their unique perspective and expressed in their unique way. We are not only drawn to messages authors want us to read, but also to the way they consistently write them.

The reason some people will camp out in front of the Apple store the night before a new product is made available is simple: It's from Apple. I would hazard to guess that many, if not most, of these same people know very little about what is new and different. They have come to expect that if it's from Apple, it's got to be great.

Each new product Apple produces is similarly linked to the one before, in design and function. The new offering may provide functional improvements, but more importantly, it remains an expression of Apple's Big-M Meaning. Apple, no doubt, takes great pains before introducing a new product to make sure that it deserves a place within the Apple family, just as the storyteller's voice is consistent story after story. Hemingway would never have written like Shakespeare, no matter how big the opportunity to sell a new Shakespearean play.

TRUST DUST

My spam folder is always good for a few laughs.

The other day, among the typical ads about increasing the size of certain body parts and/or my sexual prowess, I saw an ad for trust spray. Just spray this on a prospective client before that big meeting and the deal is as good as done. To this I say, spray a prospective client with anything, and gaining trust will be the least of your problems. Do people actually buy this stuff?

Nevertheless, this ad for some reason aroused my curiosity. I simply had to know how someone would actually attempt to sell something so ridiculous. So I clicked on the link to the trust spray website.

Once there, a seductive female avatar greeted me by announcing that now all my dreams could come true.

"Use this spray and everyone will trust you. Trust is power," she said.

I read on to discover that the magic ingredient being promoted was oxytocin, the human hormone released within our system when we experience trust.

Still curious, I clicked on the news links from ABC, NBC, and other sources that I usually perceive as credible. And as things go when I get into one of my 'just-gotta-know' jags, one link led to another and to another until I got to an abstract of the July issue of the *Journal of Psychiatry*. I was kind of busy last summer. I must have missed that issue.

Still not convinced that I ought to carry around an aerosol can of trust spray in my brief case (special pocket sizes are available too), after struggling through the journal abstract, I had to admit there was something to the oxytocin thing.

Researchers have shown that it is especially released with touch, as in a massage, and during emotional movies. In one study they showed that in both humans and dogs, oxytocin levels in the blood rose after five to twenty-four minutes of a petting session. While reading this, I'm thinking that if I engage in petting a research volunteer, I won't need trust as much as I'll need a good lawyer. Nevertheless, I am convinced that it is possible that oxytocin does play a role in the emotional bonding between humans and dogs.

For marketers, other than perhaps those trying to sell trust in a can, this raises some important questions worthy of investigation. If there is any truth to the effects of oxytocin, what does this suggest for advertising effectiveness? One might surmise that cold hard facts or opinions alone aren't going to do too much to create a bond with consumers. My guess is that very little oxytocin gets released when an ad claims superlatives for its product like "the best, the fastest, or the least expensive." Comparatively, it's easy to surmise that emotionally charged values and beliefs that are shared with the consumer can do more to create loyalty. If scientists can measure oxytocin emissions that occur through petting, certainly someone should be able to measure the flow through our bloodstream when ads take the form of stories instead of editorials. One thing for sure: It would be a lot safer.

A BRANDING LESSON FROM GEORGE ORWELL

As I walked into my office today, I found a copy of George Orwell's *1984* on my desk. I read the words "read this," with an arrow pointing to a passage on page 136. The note wasn't signed, but I could tell it was written in my assistant's handwriting.

Like most books I was supposed to read in high school, all I can remember about George Orwell's *1984* is what CliffsNotes™ told me to remember. And what I remember most are warnings against evil dictators, Big Brother, and the thought police. "Was my assistant trying to tell me something?" I wondered.

I sheepishly started reading the passage, and by the time I was done I was ready to give her a raise.

The arrow pointed to a passage about the lead character's feelings about an important book he had just read.

Orwell writes:

> The book fascinated him, or more exactly it reassured him. In a sense it told him nothing that was new, but that was part of the attraction. It said what he would have said, if it had been possible for him to set his scattered thoughts in order. It was the product of a mind similar to his own, but enormously more powerful, more systematic, less fear-ridden. **The best books, he perceived, are those that tell you what you know already.**

It was gratifying to know that at least one person was on my side. Whereas this passage refers to a book, my assistant knew that it reinforced what I believe is an important lesson that brand marketers should take away from the power of story.

Try as they might, brands, like stories, cannot change a belief if we are not ready to have that belief changed. Marketing history is rife with examples that prove the point. Oldsmobile learned this lesson the hard way when it tried to convince its audience that "This is not your father's Oldsmobile." Despite its clever attempt to shed a different light on its brand, the belief that Oldsmobile is a car for older people was too entrenched to be radicalized. As Sears learned through its efforts to shed light on the "Softer Side of Sears," it was impossible for us to let go of its harder-side image we had come to associate through brands like Craftsman, Die-Hard, and Kenmore. We laughed as Radio Shack attempted to go from geeky to hip as it told us, "You can now call us The Shack." And then there's the classic New Coke boner that taught us that changing an image, especially when it ain't broke, can be a costly mistake.

The best brands, like the best stories, are those that reinforce and clarify rather than change meaning. At its core, Old Spice is a brand we have learned to associate with masculinity. Granted, it might be our father's after shave. But "Smell Like A Man" didn't bother to change Old Spice's meaning. Rather, it stayed the course merely with a more contemporized frame of reference we now have for masculinity. Volkswagen's Beetle found its link to its reverse snobbery roots when it reestablished its cult following by introducing the new Beetle with alternative rock music. It furthered that link by attaching a flower vase to its dashboard. Sperry Topsiders, an old, tired brand sold mostly to men, dramatically increased sales by making its association with the good life, on or around the water, relevant to women and kids.

The best brands, like the best books, are those that tell us what we already know. They may tell it in a new, more relevant way, but at its heart the brand story doesn't change because it can't.

Thank you, George Orwell. And thank you, Heather.

HEY THERE! I'M TERRIFIC—
A LESSON IN STORY BRANDING

If you've gotten past the title of this essay (and many don't), you're obviously intrigued. How could anyone expect to sell anything this way? Telling someone you're terrific is so, well . . . crass, obnoxious, Neanderthal, anything but effective. Right?

Curious, I created an experiment. I set out to see how people would actually react to someone saying, "Hey there! I am terrific!" not in written words, but in a real face-to-face interaction. So, taking my life into my own hands, I stood out on a street corner to see how passersby might react to me.

After a startled stare and/or a quizzical "huh?" I either received a polite "no, thanks" or a profane description of what I should do with or to myself. Consequently, I gave up on this experiment early on, so I don't have anything that would come even close to a projectable sample. But I'm going to take a leap of faith and hypothesize that the chances of someone responding with, "Okay, I'm buying whatever terrificness you're selling" are slim to none.

So why would I do such a thing? What's to figure out? Nobody talks this way. So why care?

Before you answer that, watch a little TV tonight and pay particular attention to the commercials. Take stock of how often brands use self-praise, as in "We are reliable, we are caring, tasty, smart, cool, smooth, sexy, etc." Look around you on billboards, postcards, digital banners, restaurant place mats—wherever there is paper, video, or audio paid for by an advertiser, chances are that it won't be long before you see and hear words telling you how terrific some brand is.

Okay, so most advertising isn't quite as objectionable as some stranger walking up to a person pronouncing human superiority. Furthermore, being blatantly immodest may be frowned upon in one-on-one verbal exchanges, but it's totally acceptable for advertisers. You with me so far?

I recently visited my doctor for a routine physical and my annual guilt trip for loving an occasional cigar. When I called to make an appointment, the operator made it sound like she was upset because I'd interrupted a winning hand of Solitaire. She put me on hold while she looked up my information. There, in phone purgatory, I heard three of the hospital's latest commercials delivered by somebody I didn't know (or trust) telling me that at this particular hospital, "EXCELLENCE IS ALL AROUND YOU."

"How about that?" I thought. In the twenty-some years I've been coming to this place, it never occurred to me that excellence was all around me. I thought all along that this health care center that I went to for the sake of staying alive was just mediocre. Gave me goosebumps.

When I arrived for the appointment, I saw posters and brochures tagged "Excellence is All Around You." Then, when I got the "you're healthy" email from my doctor, the very same advertising tag line was placed under his signature. I like my doctor (except for the cigar lectures). I like the hospital he's affiliated with. I wouldn't think of switching. But it has absolutely nothing to do with his or the hospital's self-serving opinion that "excellence is all around me," even if it is. I decide what's excellent, what's cool, what's "terrific"—not the advertiser. It's actually insulting. But if I started feeling insulted every time I was exposed to advertising like this, I would need to book another appointment with a different kind of doctor, for depression.

Why, then, one might wonder, do we advertise this way? Could it be that it's always done this way, that it's culturally acceptable for advertisers to brag and boast about who they are and what they do? We ignore most of it anyway, so who cares?

If you have a brand, and especially now that the social media is allowing people to share truths about it, and apart from your self-promoting bias, you maybe ought to care. What's the solution? I asked this of some astute marketing people recently, and their answer was to rely more on facts than opinions or puffed-up superiority claims. "Let the facts speak for themselves," they said. Okay, I'm cool with that. Seems logical. But even hard, cold, provable facts have their foibles.

Last summer, we conducted a study of an ad for a client promoting the "fact" that it had just been recognized by J.D. Powers for having the "best customer satisfaction" as compared to its competitors. Surprisingly, it generated little or no positive response. Here were some of the things respondents told us:

"J.D. Powers is not me. How do they know what I'm looking for?" "Did [the advertiser] pay for this award?" "Doesn't do anything for me." "Yeah, but what aren't they telling us?"

This is not to say that a brand fortunate enough to garner a third-party endorsement like this should keep it hidden from consumers. But it does suggest that facts alone do not always outperform claims of superiority.

So, let's sum it up here. We can't brag. And facts aren't as hardworking as one might think. Is my purpose here to completely destroy the institution of advertising on which so much depends (including my living)? Am I out of my mind? Absolutely not, and I'm pleading the fifth on that second question.

Some brands have actually found the solution. Besides the usual suspects like Nike, Apple, and Harley-Davidson, North Face provides a great example with its "Never Stop Exploring" campaign. Then there's Corona's "Find Your Beach" and Chipotle's "Cultivate a Better World." If you look closely, you won't find one declarative "we" in ideas expressed by these brands—no brags, no boasts—just a clearly stated value or belief in what is important. And by association with these beliefs, these brands tell an important story about themselves without getting in their own way. Through these expressions, these brands say volumes about who they are without explanation.

These are what I refer to as "StoryBrands." I call them that because they function the way stories do. Stories don't push influence on us; they pull us in. They create rather than force identification. They create resonance to the extent that we share the underlying belief that is espoused.

Gaining trust is everything when it comes to persuasion. And when you are the one trying to gain trust, credibility is influenced by many other factors besides what you think of yourself or an endorsement by a credible source. Thinking of your brand as its main story character with a cause or a reason for being, one that goes beyond the profit motive, can open up new, more creative alternatives for advertisers than the old standby "brag and boast" form of persuasion. Instead of being the hospital that brags "excellence is all around you," perhaps an association with the value of excellence as a worthwhile pursuit in life, let alone health care, would be a more effective appeal. Instead of being the brand that cites some statistic about customer satisfaction, perhaps an association with the shared value of people caring for other people would render greater trust. As such, story logic provides an important remedy for advertising at a time when consumer skepticism and distrust are mounting.

We were humans before we became consumers. As humans, we naturally gravitate to stories and the ideas, experiences, and lessons with which they invite us to participate.

Speaking of lessons, I only have two. Think of your brand as a story, not a braggart. And don't try my experiment at home.

WANT THE JOB? TELL A STORY

Jack and David were finalists for the same job. Both had relevant experience and equally impressive resumes. Following their final interviews, the executives who had met with both of them convened to evaluate each candidate separately.

Jack received high praise from the executives. He was smart, accomplished, and personable. But when the discussion turned to David, one of the executives got up from his seat and walked to the front of the room. Looking across the conference room table he said, "Okay, put your pencils down for this one. I just have to tell you about my interview with David."

The room went silent in anticipation of what he was going to say.

"So, along with all the other stuff I usually ask in interviews, I decided to do something different. I flat out asked David to convince me that he was a strong motivator. He looked a little startled at first.

"'What do you mean?' he asked.

"'C'mon,' I said. 'A sales manager should be a good salesman. Surely you can sell yourself.'"

The executive continued. "And with that, David looked down as he paused for a few seconds gathering his thoughts. And just as I was starting to think he was about to stumble, he spoke up.

"'I know that you need to develop your sales force,' David said. 'And it only makes sense that you need someone who is a strong motivator. Can I tell you a little story?'

"'Do whatever you want,' I answered. 'Just convince me you know how to motivate people.'

"And so, he told me about a time when he had to deal with an employee whose performance was lacking. He explained how surprised he was to see this employee's sales performance fall off from his normally expected level. He went on to tell me that he told this employee that he was very concerned.

"'I told him I was concerned for the company,' David said. 'But I also explained that I was a little worried about him. We talked for a while until he opened up to me.'

"David then went on to tell me that his employee had been distracted because of some family issues. Without going into detail, he let David in on some of the circumstances he was facing.

"'I merely listened without giving advice,' David continued. 'And I ended our discussion by telling him that I would help him in any way I could. I then expressed my belief in his value to the company. There wasn't a big turnaround at first. But it didn't take too long before he exceeded everyone's expectations, I think even his own.'

"There was a long pause. I wasn't overly impressed," the executive remarked.

"'If you're telling me that it takes a little understanding to motivate people,' I said, 'then you're telling me something that I would expect from anyone applying for this job.'

"'But with all due respect, that's not what I'm saying, sir.'

"'Okay,' I told him. 'Then I must be missing the point.'

"He looked straight at me, moving up in his seat, and then he said something that blew me away.

"'It's one thing to motivate employees by understanding them,' he said. 'But it's quite another to let them know they are *worth* understanding.'

"I sat back in my seat and thought, 'Wow!' Typically, when I ask candidates to convince me of anything, they give me some sort of brag, or suggest that I talk to a former boss or employee for corroboration. But this guy didn't do that. He didn't promote himself. I didn't get the long-winded self-assessment I expected. Rather, he showed me what I wanted to see by sharing a relevant experience. If that's how he persuades people to adopt his point of view, my vote is to get David on our team."

The rest of the executives concurred. David got the job.

The Power of Stories

One of the reasons stories are so powerful is that they go beyond reporting factual results. Instead, they reveal beliefs and values that are responsible for the results. Through the power of story, David engaged his listener by involving him in an experience that demonstrated the way he thinks.

Stories that are relevant and well told will always help interviewers get more of what they're looking for.

THE MIDAZ CLUTCH

MIDAZ was revolutionizing the music industry. Unlike anything before it, this new software platform was allowing music writers to eliminate the need for a computer keyboard. All commands could now be directed solely by touching designated piano keys. Besides receiving rave reviews, sales were through the roof.

Then, almost like someone flipped a switch, the parade of inbound orders was cut in half when a new competitor came on the scene. VoiceKontrol* introduced software that performed similar functions, but through voice commands. MIDAZ quickly reacted with advertising that explained how much easier their software was to set up and learn. The company aggressively promoted the fact that, with MIDAZ, no microphone was needed and that keyboard touch commands were far more accurate than their less reliable voice-command counterparts. In their ads, MIDAZ even showed itself surpassing VoiceKontrol in a battery of third-party tests measuring speed, ease, and accuracy. But despite all this, MIDAZ's month-to-month sales growth declined and margins continued to shrink as MIDAZ was forced to lower its price to remain competitive.

The owner of MIDAZ turned to a branding consultant for advice. Upon evaluating the situation, the expert reminded the owner of Einstein's theory of insanity, the one about continuing to do the same thing despite getting the same results.

"But we HAVE changed our approach," the owner complained. "Haven't you seen our ads that show third-party test results?"

"Obviously, considering your sales situation, your customers don't seem to care about test results."

The consultant went on to explain that MIDAZ was no longer new and different, thanks to a competitor who was offering an acceptable substitute.

---

* No brands were hurt during the writing of this article. MIDAZ and VoiceKontrol are fictitious.

"In the beginning, all you had to do was sell the logic behind your product's advantages," the consultant explained. "But now, facts are no longer enough. Regardless of whether your product is superior to the competition's, the rules of the game have changed. And unless you rise above this 'mine is better than yours' comparison war, you're still the leader. And leaders don't typically chase followers."

"Okay, then, what do I do?" pleaded the owner.

"Let me come back in a week, and I'll explain what I mean."

One week later, the consultant returned.

"I'm going to give you a sentence that will provide a new roadmap for your brand," the consultant said. "But before I show you what I've written, I need to remind you of some things you already know. For instance, I need to remind you that you started out as a musician. And because you saw the need to help people just like you make the most of their talents, you came up with an easy-to-use software platform. I need to remind you that what you stand for isn't your product; it's your belief that musicians shouldn't have to become computer geeks. And, I need to remind you that this belief is what constantly motivates you to find even better ways to help musicians realize their full potential."

"Okay, consider me reminded," said the president.

"And with that, you need to see that associating with this belief is what is going to make you more unique than any new feature you add today or tomorrow or next year, features that your competitors will eventually react to or copy."

Then the consultant held up a piece of paper. And on that paper were the words:

SINCE WHEN HAS PLAYING BECOME WORK?

"So, is this what they call a unique selling proposition?" asked the president.

"No," answered the consultant. "Your unique selling proposition is what you've been advertising. It consists of all those facts you are trying to sell. But clearly, this hasn't been enough to regain lost market share."

"Is this a new ad headline?"

"No," answered the consultant.

"A new tag line?"

"Not quite," said the consultant.

As the president sat staring at the piece of paper, the consultant asked him who in his audience would disagree with this statement.

"Nobody, really," he answered.

"Exactly," he said.

"You see, you don't need a new, unique selling proposition as much as you need a unique *value* proposition, something that represents the value or belief you stand for. And that's what this sentence is. A unique selling proposition might help you sell your church, but having and demonstrating your unique value proposition will help you sell your religion."

"What do you mean?" asked the president.

"Certainly you need buyers. But what you really need are followers—people who relate to your cause because it's their cause. And followers help spread the word faster than buyers do. Demonstrate the meaning of this sentence in everything you do, and I assure you things will change for the better."

The president took the expert's advice. Instead of solely relying on boastful, here-today-copied-tomorrow claims about product superiority, he started to find ways to bring his unique value proposition to life. And soon his targets started seeing MIDAZ as a cause, more than a brand of music-writing software. The owner started providing social media content that would help musicians more easily write music. He started conducting contests among users for the best music-writing tips. He set up forums and Wikis for musicians to share ideas with each other. And the new thrust of his advertising helped prospects relate to the MIDAZ brand as the one that understood them, the one to which they could relate. And sales starting taking off once again as MIDAZ started regaining lost market share.

THE LESSON

As brands mature, competitors will start to steal market share with substitutes. Whenever this happens, it is especially important to start associating your brand with a cause or a value that will resonate with your targets.

Certainly, promoting your product differences will remain important. But they need the help of your unique value proposition in order to stand out. Your unique value proposition defines the driving motivation behind your brand's existence.

Before it's too late, define yours.

WHAT'S ALL THE BUZZ AMONG MARKETERS ABOUT STORYTELLING?

Okay. Sell with stories. I get it. They work better than explicit hit-them-over-the-head-and-kick-them-in-the-behind-fact-based-and-really-boring selling messages. Stories don't push influence. They pull influence. People become more engaged with stories. Done. Got it.

The fact is that story-based messaging has been around since before "Does She or Doesn't She?" Nothing new. Just do more of it. Again, point well taken.

Storytelling and StoryBranding are two very different things. Knowing the difference is critically important.

First and foremost, storytelling is a tactic. It's a tool that furthers acceptance of certain claims and invites involvement and memorability. And it's a very useful tool when and if it can be used (hard to tell a story on a billboard or a banner ad). But there is a very big difference between telling a story to sell something and actually becoming the story itself. The difference between the two is the difference between merely using examples or metaphors to make a point and actually becoming the example of a value worth subscribing to.

Storytelling illuminates a selling point through some plot line that puts an audience in the shoes of a fictitious or very real character. In contrast, StoryBranding occurs when the brand itself takes on the role of lead character, who embodies beliefs that are shared with its audience. Okay, both storytelling and StoryBranding draw on the power and principles of story. But StoryBranding is a planning process that helps brand marketers better articulate and define the foundational beliefs that their brands are built upon and the values that sustain them over time.

Let's break it down a little differently. When you think like a StoryBrander (we're working on the secret handshake), you think like an author who needs to share something important with the world. But instead of developing a plot with an important theme or message, you are promoting a way to solve a problem within the context of an important worldview. Your brand corroborates your professed worldview through any and all products or services that bear its name. Thus StoryBranding is a strategy, not a tactic, deployed to keep the plot and theme supporting each other. On the other hand, storytelling is usually relegated to the presentation of plots alone.

Thinking in terms of opposites can help here. You can see plenty of StoryBranding opposites perusing through those in-flight gadget catalogs that come in handy when you have to put away anything with an on/off switch—the ones promoting plasticene necktie protectors, shoe lifts, and those lap pillows the size of a beer keg "ideal" for napping on the plane (does anybody actually use these?).

If an ad is shouting "Glory hallelujah, there IS a better mousetrap," it is probably not a StoryBrand. These ads are exclusively about function without regard for brand, or in story terms, all plot and no theme. Story-Brands, in addition to presenting a unique solution to a given problem, also encourage their audiences to believe in something bigger than the product. "Think Different," "Just Do It," and "Never Stop Exploring" are classic StoryBrand themes. In addition to communicating beliefs or values that are strongly subscribed to by the makers of the brand, they explain why the brand exists beyond its profit motive. And they provide one with confidence that the product presented, much like other products that bear its brand name, is indeed a better mousetrap.

And so, StoryBrands promote causes, in addition to claims. Well-differentiated and newsworthy claims are a good thing. Just keep in mind that a claim without a cause is a car without an engine. Consumers want to know why they should buy from you just as much as they want to know about what it is they are buying.

Storytelling is a very effective way to open eyes to the problems your product solves. StoryBranding does that, too, but gets to the heart of why your brand exists.

References and Suggested Reading

Bedbury, Scott, and Stephen Fenichell. *A New Brand World: 8 Principles for Achieving Brand Leadership in the 21st Century*. New York: Viking, 2002.

Blanding, Michael. *The Coke Machine: The Dirty Truth Behind the World's Favorite Soft Drink*. New York: Avery, 2010.

Denning, Stephen. *The Springboard: How Storytelling Ignites Action in Knowledge-Era Organizations*. Boston: Butterworth-Heinemann, 2001.

Ferrell, William K. *Literature and Film as Modern Mythology*. Praeger Paperback, 2000.

Gabriel, Yiannis. *Myths, Stories, and Organizations: Premodern Narratives for Our Times*. New York: Oxford University Press, 2004.

Godin, Seth. *All Marketers Are Liars: The Power of Telling Authentic Stories in a Low-Trust World*. New York: Portfolio, 2005.

Godin, Seth. *Tribes: We Need You to Lead Us*. Brilliance Audio on MP3-CD, 2008.

Hanlon, Patrick. *Primal Branding: Create Zealots for Your Brand, Your Company, and Your Future*. New York: Free Press, 2006.

Haven, Kendall F. *Story Proof: The Science Behind the Startling Power of Story*. Westport, CT: Libraries Unlimited, 2007.

King, Stephen. *On Writing: A Memoir of the Craft*. New York: Scribners, 2010.

Lakhani, Dave. *Persuasion: The Art of Getting What You Want*. Wiley, 2005.

Lipman, Doug. *Improving Your Storytelling: Beyond the Basics for All Who Tell Stories in Work or Play*. Little Rock, AR: August House, 1999.

Margolis, Michael. *Believe Me: Why Your Vision, Brand, and Leadership Need a Bigger Story*. New York: Get Storied Press, 2009.

Mark, Margaret, and Carol Pearson. *The Hero and the Outlaw: Building Extraordinary Brands Through the Power of Archetypes*. New York: McGraw-Hill, 2001.

Mathews, Ryan, and Watts Wacker. *What's Your Story?: Storytelling to Move Markets, Audiences, People, and Brands*. Upper Saddle River, NJ: FT Press, 2008.

Maxwell, Richard, and Robert Dickman. *The Elements of Persuasion: Use Storytelling to Pitch Better, Sell Faster, & Win More Business*. 1st ed. New York: Collins, 2007.

McKee, Robert. *Story: Substance, Structure, Style, and the Principles of Screenwriting*. 1st ed. New York: ReganBooks, 1997.

Naisbitt, John. *Megatrends: Ten New Directions Transforming Our Lives*. New York: Warner Books, 1982.

Pink, Daniel H. *A Whole New Mind: Why Right-Brainers Will Rule the Future*. New York: Riverhead Trade (Paperbacks), 2006.

Porter, Michael E. *On Competition*. Updated and expanded ed. Boston: Harvard Business School Pub., 2008.

Reeves, Rosser. *Reality in Advertising* [1st Borzoi ed.]. New York: Knopf, 1961.

Reiman, Joey. *The Story of Purpose*. NJ: Wiley and Sons, 2013.

Simmons, Annette. *The Story Factor: Inspiration, Influence, and Persuasion Through the Art of Storytelling*. New York: Basic Books, 2001.

Simmons, Annette. *Whoever Tells the Best Story Wins: How to Use Your Own Stories to Communicate with Power and Impact*. New York: Amacom, 2007.

Smith, Logan Pearsall. *Afterthoughts*. London: Constable, 1931.

Vincent, Laurence. *Legendary Brands: Unleashing the Power of Storytelling to Create a Winning Marketing Strategy*. Chicago: Dearborn Trade Pub., 2002.

My Story

I've always had a passion for advertising. My favorite assignment in grade school was "show and tell." As a paperboy, I would add subscribers by copy testing leaflets. ("If you buy from me, I promise not to throw your paper in the bushes" outranked "You need the news; I need the money.")

After receiving both a BA and an MA in advertising from Michigan State University, I started my adult career in advertising in nearby Chicago. I later worked in New York, Los Angeles, and Baltimore gaining experience on a wide variety of major accounts like Citibank, Kraft Foods, Burger King, General Electric, Toshiba, Arby's, the American Marketing Association, and many others.

In 1999 I decided I was crazy enough to make a difference against the backdrop of some 3000 other advertising agencies in the US. I started my own agency in Chicago that today goes by the name eswStoryLab. The agency was started with three people and a great deal of adrenaline. Over time, we grew to becoming recognized by *Inc. Magazine* as one of the fastest-growing independent companies in the US.

While running the agency, a number of us became interested in the power of story. We set out to understand why stories are so powerful and how advertising can benefit from the way they work as a persuasive device. And through our learnings, we found our purpose. We discovered that the biggest difference we can make is in helping brands find their stories, much the same way we found ours. Thinking of a brand as a shared belief or value that will foster strong and enduring relationships is much more effective than thinking of a brand solely in terms of its unique selling proposition.

When I'm not working on finding or telling a brand's story, I am an avid golfer, tennis player, and drummer. I'm also the owner of a prized Pez collection. I live with Joan, my wife, best friend, and creative muse, in Evanston, Illinois.

For more information and to inquire about
speaking engagements,
go to www.jimsignorelli.com
or email Jim.Signorelli@eswstorylab.com

If you enjoyed this book, tell your local library about it
so that it can be shared with others.

INDEX

www.ingramcontent.com/pod-product-compliance
Lightning Source LLC
Chambersburg PA
CBHW030455210326
41597CB00013B/677